FROM TERRACED HOUSES TO RESIDENTIAL ESTATES

THE sub/URBAN IDEA

The Deutsche Nationalbibliothek lists this publication in
the Deutsche Nationalbibliografie; detailed bibliographic
data are available on the Internet at http://dnb.dnb.de

ISBN 978-3-03768-214-2
© 2017 by Braun Publishing AG
www.braun-publishing.ch

1st edition 2017

Editor: Editorial Office van Uffelen
Editorial staff and layout: Katrin Bühner, Fanny Klang,
Nora Meyer, Anne-Sophie Müller
Translation: Cosima Talhouni
Graphic concept: Michaela Prinz, Berlin
Reproduction: Bild1Druck GmbH, Berlin

LISA BAKER

FROM TERRACED HOUSES TO RESIDENTIAL ESTATES

THE sub/URBAN IDEA

CONTENTS

MIXED DEVELOPMENTS

PREFACE
SPACE FOR LIVING

In times of increasing need for living space in metropolises, the construction of residential complexes and housing estates is becoming more and more important. Living space in inner cities is becoming scarce and constantly more expensive, the number of unused plots is decreasing and the price/performance ratio and quantity of the small remaining areas are not capable of meeting the demand. Only construction across several connected plots makes

generation of socially committed architects demanded, initially independent of a specific style, the return to perimeter block development, the mixed use of quarters, and, especially, increased urban density. Team X (1953–1981) modified the urban planning postulates of the "Congrès International d'Architecture Moderne" (CIAM, Charter of Athens, 1928) and demanded the return of neighborhoods and functional diversity. In contin-

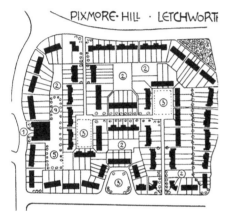

it possible to create affordable living space in the vicinity of cities – either in the outskirts or on premises that previously served other purposes. While a few years ago this mainly involved the conversion of huge areas, such as former industrial harbors, today's residential complexes consist of smaller units on the premises of abandoned factories, or warehouses that are also no longer used due to the large conversions or subsequent densification.

The experiences gained in post-war modernity in the 1960s and 1970s already showed that large settlements often turned into social trouble hotspots. This is why since the 1980s at the latest there was a rethinking process that split even larger complexes into smaller units. Such smaller units can not only be implemented on green field areas on the outskirts of cities but also integrated in the remnants of urban structures.

To avoid repetition of the errors of loosely structured complexes or even satellite towns, a new

uation of this concept and sometimes overdoing it, post-modernity evolved in the 1980s into the dominating style of New Urbanism which prospered in the USA and that declared small towns and suburbia as the ideal residential styles. In 1993 this movement was institutionalized with the "Congress for the New Urbanism" (CNU) and in 1996 its demands were put in writing in the "Charter of the New Urbanism." The choice of the words congress and charter already indicated that it was deliberately opposed to classical modernity and the post-war modernity that evolved from it. One of the first prototype manifestations of this movement was Seaside in Florida (1979, Robert S. Davis). It replicated the idolized ideal of American small towns in a new, and in part excellent, architecture. However, soon there was resistance to this as well and it was no coincidence that Seaside was chosen as the location of the movie "The Truman Show" (1998, Peter Weir) – when the keyword "globalization" gained ground during the 1990s, such an idyllic world was considered to be naïve and the retro style outdated. Nowadays this building genre has taken on a completely new look. The key characteristic of modern residential complexes is that they are constructed in the vicinity of the city and merged into the metropolitan area. The time of projects in the outskirts, whether as satellite cities or New Urbanism, is definitely over. While there is still demand for individual neighborhoods, they

designed according to a related design, we consider it to be a connected residential complex. These can consist of apartment buildings, which are usually grouped in groups of three to five, or single-family homes, as well as row houses. The conglomeration of several such complexes in a quarter is mainly an urban development task. The smaller complexes that emerge today usually resort to already existing infrastructures, and are thus incorporat-

are sought after in the city. The focus is again on diversity as already demanded by Team X. Large settlements on the outskirts of cities are often broken up into smaller units and developed based on various designs. While a uniform look is ensured by the building plans and esthetic guidelines, they nevertheless lack the standard building styles based on a single or limited designs, which was the main characteristic of housing estates even before the concept of the garden city emerged. Therefore, this is no longer estate construction as described by this book, but rather a collection of unique buildings or often individual complexes on a larger area. Only when several buildings are

ed into existing urban structures. A major focus is on the access ways, especially the separation of vehicle and pedestrian traffic. Offsetting and buildings with gradate heights create individual spaces on the inside and the outside. The examples presented in this book present the whole diversity that emerges from this current understanding of residential complexes. Texts explain both the architectural aspects as well as the urban planning characteristics and the short explanations by the architects could serve as the basis of a new "charter of residential complex construction in the 21st century."

Barry Parker and Raymond Unwin: Pixmore-Hill project in Letchworth Garden City, England, 1904.
Mackay Hugh Baillie Scott: Semi-detached cottages for Letchworth Garden City, England, 1905.
Fuggerei in Augsburg, Germany: The worlds oldest social housing estate still in use, founded by Jakob Fugger the Younger, 1516 (picture credit: Slick / wikimedia commons).
Ludwig Mies van der Rohe: 24 Apartments Weißenhofsiedlung 1–4 in Stuttgart, Germany, 1927 (picture credit: Andreas Praefcke / wikimedia commons).

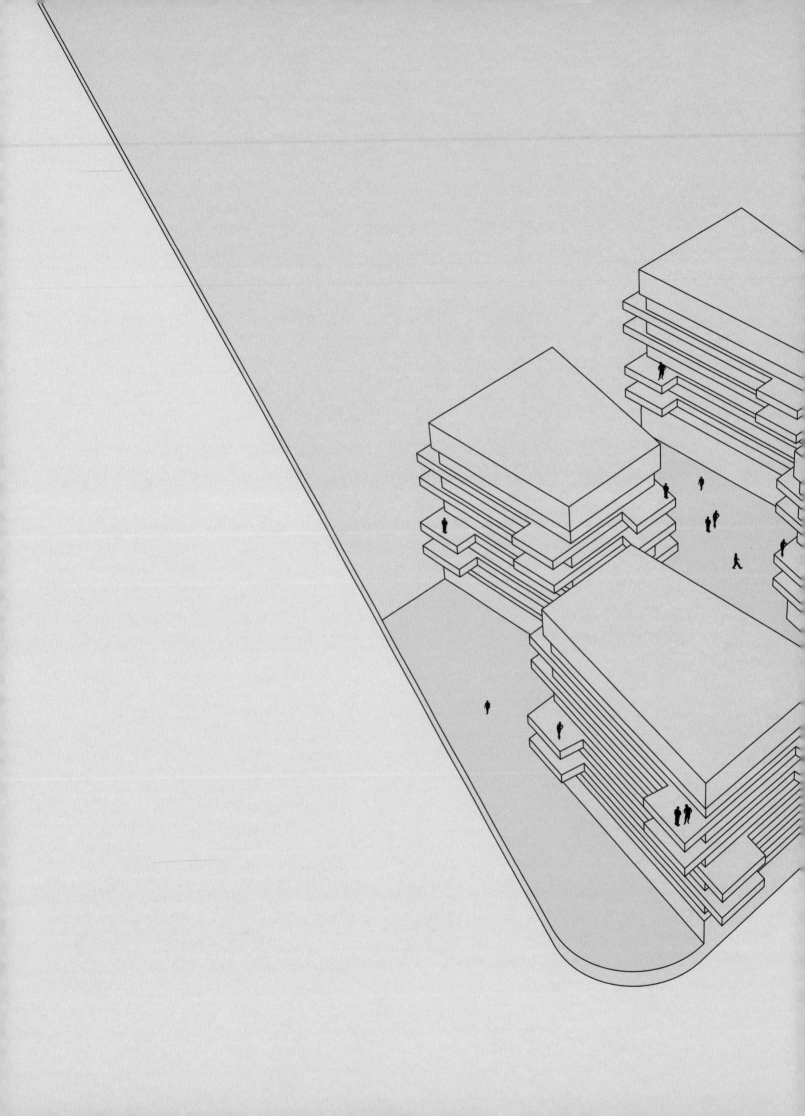

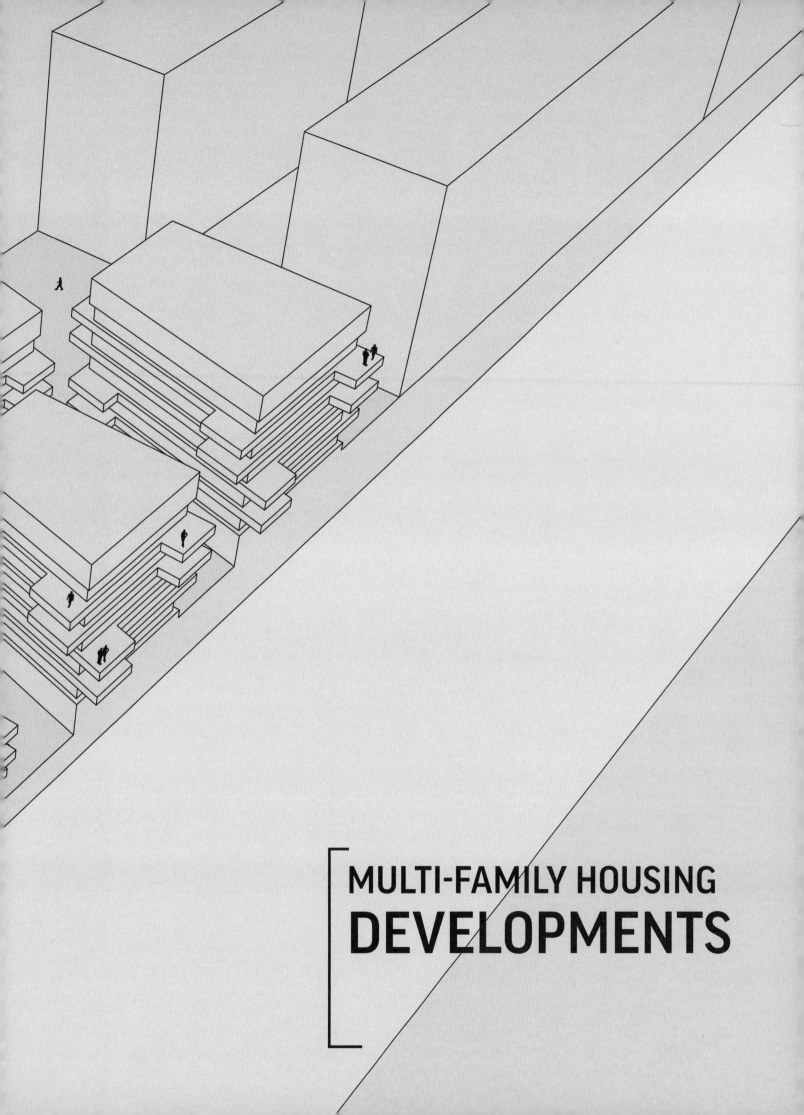

MULTI-FAMILY HOUSING
DEVELOPMENTS

ULUS SAVOY RESIDENCES
EAA EMRE AROLAT ARCHITECTURE

LOCATION: ADNAN SAYGUN CAD. 66, 34347 ULUS İSTANBUL, TURKEY | **COMPLETION:** 2013 | **CLIENT:** ÇARMIKLI AND SARUHAN | **PHOTOGRAPHER:** CEMAL EMDEN

The legal requirements defined quite rigidly the massive structure of the blocks to be built, such as the 15-by-20-meter base area that had to be parallel to the slope of the lot, the projections on stories above the ground floor, and the roofs with a 33-percent slope on all four sides. In addition, Ulus Valley is crowded with construction projects due to the many gated communities all built under the above-mentioned conditions. Despite all these unfavorable factors, the Savoy project's location within the city, the dynamic structure of its topography, and the investor's rigid attitude regarding the architectural prerequisites, the project was inspiring and heartening. The garage level was given precedence as one of the main conditioning elements of the design. By focusing on its top cover, it constituted the substructure of a new topography within a negative-positive relationship. Each level in the garage was connected by ramps, rendering it fluid. Some of the shells that formed the cover were completely removed; occasional slits and interstices formed by the slight difference in levels between two shells created surprising nuances that blurred the boundary between the underground layer and the exterior. These nuances allow daylight to penetrate the shell and connect recreational areas to the exterior. At night, they can also illuminate the landscape thanks to the light that seeps out from the inside.

FACTS
SITE SIZE: 59,900 SQM
GFA TOTAL: 83,000 SQM
NO. BUILDINGS: 26
NO. UNITS: 304
ROAD LENGTH: 285 M
KIND OF UNITS: 4 TYPES 101–341 SQM
556 UNDERGROUND PARKING LOTS

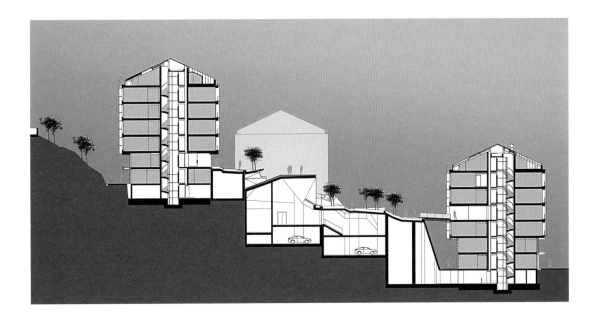

There were two important sources of input regarding this settlement located in Ulus, Turkey, which was planned as 26 identically sized units for many, approximately 80,000 square meters. The first of these was the rigidity of building conditions that apply to these regions of the city. The second was having to cope with a project that was prepared beforehand, whose intricate processes of approval were already legally completed, and to whose outlines the investor preferred to adhere to within this context. Although all architectural decisions were shaped almost solely by conforming to operative building conditions, keeping the number, location, and heights of building blocks in the new design exactly as those in the existing project was another key requirement.

RECOGNITION

SHELLS, WHICH ARE THE MAIN MATERIAL OF THE LOCAL LANDSCAPE, ARE AN IMPORTANT CHARACTERISTIC OF THE SETTLEMENT. THEY ARE PRESENT IN ALL THEIR HARDNESS AND SHARPNESS. THOUGH MOST OFTEN PARTLY CONCEALED BY THE LAYER OF VEGETATION GROWING OVER THEM, THEY REMAIN VISIBLE ONE WAY OR ANOTHER FROM ALL POINTS OF THE AREA.

ROSENBÜCHEL
BAUMSCHLAGER EBERLE

LOCATION: ROSENBÜCHELSTRASSE, 9014 ST. GALLEN, SWITZERLAND | **COMPLETION:** 2007, 2010 AND 2011 | **CLIENT:** SWISS LIFE ZURICH (1ST AND 2ND PHASE), SENN BPM, ZURICH (3RD PHASE) | **LANDSCAPE ARCHITECTS:** ROTZLER KREBS PARTNER GMBH | **PHOTOGRAPHER:** EDUARD HUEBER, ARCH PHOTO, INC.

The individual buildings, which were designed in a villa style, contain rental apartments of various sizes in multi-story triplets. This creates considerable density while saving space and valuable resource ground. At the same time, neighborhoods emerge that are supported by individual connection paths in the territory. The complex is undoubtedly intended as a realistic alternative to the popular single-family dwelling agglomerations whose primary "quality" – extensive space requirement – is no longer acceptable today. The sustainable handling of the terrain is also reflected in the façades that were designed for longevity. Differences in the by now four construction stages of the settlement can be seen. In the first stage, exposed brickwork was used, followed by superimposed clinker, which has been replaced by noble natural rock in the most recent stage. The structure of the façades also introduces movement. Instead of strict symmetry, there is a low-key interplay of varying open and closed sections and elements.

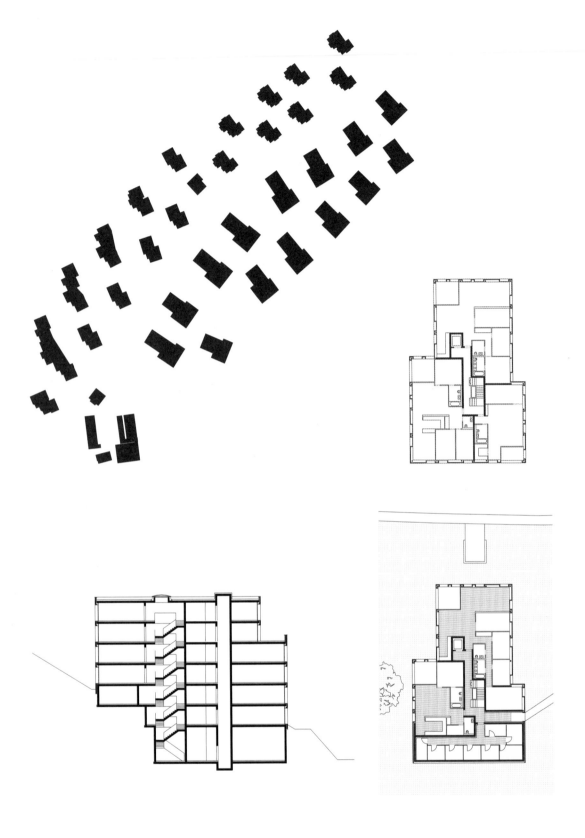

The Rosenbüchel settlement is located at the interception between the periphery of the Swiss regional capital of St. Gallen and its rural surroundings. Its point houses are prominent accents in the topography of the steep rock slope. The compact buildings counter the contour lines of the slope. However, they do not follow a strictly stereometric pattern, which, similar to the architecture, highlights the civilizing intervention. The horizontal incorporation into the landscape not only incorporates the settlement into its surroundings, but also enables excellent views from the individual houses.

DIFFICULT TERRAIN

THE SUSTAINABLE HANDLING OF THE TERRAIN IS EVIDENT NOT ONLY IN THE FAÇADES. THE ROSENBÜCHEL SETTLEMENT ALSO OFFERS ITS RESIDENTS CUSTOMIZED OUTDOOR AREAS INCLUDING LOGGIAS, TERRACES, AND PATHS THROUGHOUT THE COMPLEX.

FACTS

SITE SIZE: 32,200 SQM
GFA TOTAL: 17,800 SQM
NO. BUILDINGS: 14
NO. UNITS: 158
ROAD LENGTH: 330 M
KIND OF UNITS: 1–6 BEDROOMS
288 UNDERGROUND PARKING
LOTS

NEUES WOHNEN BRUNOSTRASSE
STEFAN FORSTER ARCHITEKTEN

LOCATION: MICHELSTRASSE 1, BRUNOSTRASSE 4-14, 97082 WÜRZBURG, GERMANY |
COMPLETION: 2012 | **CLIENT:** STADTBAU WÜRZBURG GMBH | **PHOTOGRAPHER:** LISA
FARKAS

The residential compound in the Zellerau district of Würzburg, which was incorporated into the urban planning support program "Die soziale Stadt" (the social city) in 2007, replaces conventional row houses of the 1950s, similar to the ones that can still be seen to the south of the new buildings. Nine rectangular individual houses, each containing 10–15 apartments are offset to each other and allow the preservation of the distinctive ancient trees among them. The positioning of the houses creates a park-like varied landscape and constitutes an urban development connection among the different construction structures surrounding the complex. With its social mix of supported and freely financed apartments, the complex has created a new benchmark for residential construction in Würzburg. It consists of 42 condominiums, 50 rental and 12 social housing apartments with two to five rooms ranging from 46 to 142 square meters. The individual apartment furnishings and full handicap accessibility additionally contribute to the socially upgraded and newly mixed city quarter. The larger apartments are aligned in three directions, while the available car sharing offer significantly reduces the number of required parking spots.

FACTS

SITE SIZE: 10,570 SQM
GFA TOTAL: 10,675 SQM
NO. BUILDINGS: 9
NO. UNITS: 104
APARTMENTS: 1-4 BEDROOMS
65 UNDERGROUND PARKING LOTS
CAR SHARING FACILITIES

Originally built in the 1950s in the western part of the city of Würzburg and based on the urban structure of decentralized cities that was prevalent at the time, the Zellerau complex is dominated by rows of three-story apartment buildings with simple standards. A special feature are the large leisure and greened areas with old trees that are worthy of conservation. The city quarter had been neglected for many years to the detriment of its image. This was one of the reasons why it was in-cluded in the federal and local urban development support program for city quarters with particular development needs in 2007.

NATURAL CONNECTION

DUE TO THE CONSISTENT PRESERVATION OF THE EXISTING NATURAL STRUCTURE, ESPECIALLY THE LARGE TREES, THE NEW BUILDINGS ARE CONNECTED AS A MATTER OF COURSE WITH THE ROW HOUSES QUARTER BORDERING IT TO THE SOUTH.

LIVING LEO
ARCHITEKTENKONTOR FALLER + KRÜCK

LOCATION: LEONARDO-DA-VINCI-ALLEE 12, 60486 FRANKFURT/MAIN, GERMANY |
COMPLETION: 2016 | **CLIENT:** FORMART GMBH & CO KG | **OPEN SPACE DESIGN:** PLAN °D |
PHOTOGRAPHER: FRANK DEINHARD

Situated on an almost perfectly square plot of land, this residential complex appears from the outside to be a completely closed-off block. From the center courtyard, however, it presents itself as airy and open due to the wide gaps in the corners of the block.

Six of the eight houses are grouped as high rows extending from east to west while two point houses with two floors less enclose the northern and southern sides. Most apartments face west with large balconies for enjoying the evening sun. A second balcony attached to the bedrooms on the east side enhances the apartments, while creating a varied interior courtyard façade. Oriels divide the street façades into individual buildings.

Positioning the staircases inside the buildings left enough façade area to equip most apartments with windowed bathrooms.

The stairs and elevators are laterally offset from each other, creating an interesting spatial structure that can accommodate up to four apartments per floor. All parking is moved to an underground garage that is accessible through the staircase. The inner courtyard contains open areas next to shared seating and playgrounds, offering many opportunities for interaction. Independent access from the courtyard including doorbells on the doors facing it further emphasize its importance.

FACTS
SITE SIZE: 5,000 SQM
GFA TOTAL: 18,300 SQM
NO. BUILDINGS: 8
NO. UNITS: 167
ROAD LENGTH: 290 M
KIND OF UNITS: 1-4 BEDROOMS
169 UNDERGROUND PARKING LOTS

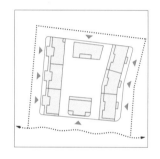
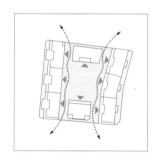
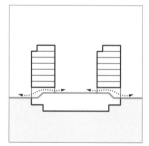
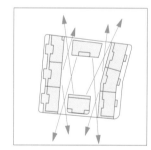

The project is located in the planning area "Am Rebstock" in Bockenheim, a very central and the most densely populated district of Frankfurt. Until the mid-1930s, the "Rebstock" premises contained Frankfurt's first airport, a fact that is still reflected in some of the quarter's streets that bear the names of German flight pioneers. The buildings in the planning areas are folded in three dimensions. The design breaks the block edge into two rows and two points and the folding of the plot is visible up to the inner courtyard. A public passage was created along the outside of the building rows with an additional passage on the inside. Inside, the courtyard presents many fascinating views of the surroundings while from the distance the complex looks like a closed-off block. Closer up, the gaps open up and the semi-public passages dissect the block, revealing the permeable structure of semi-public and private outdoor areas.

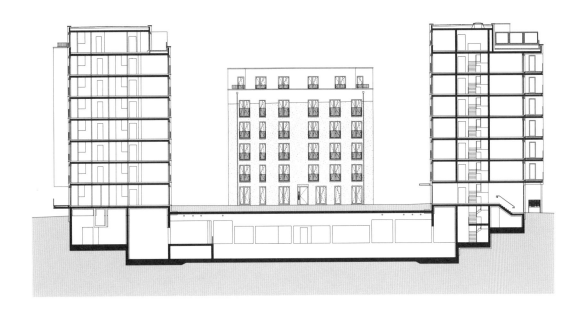

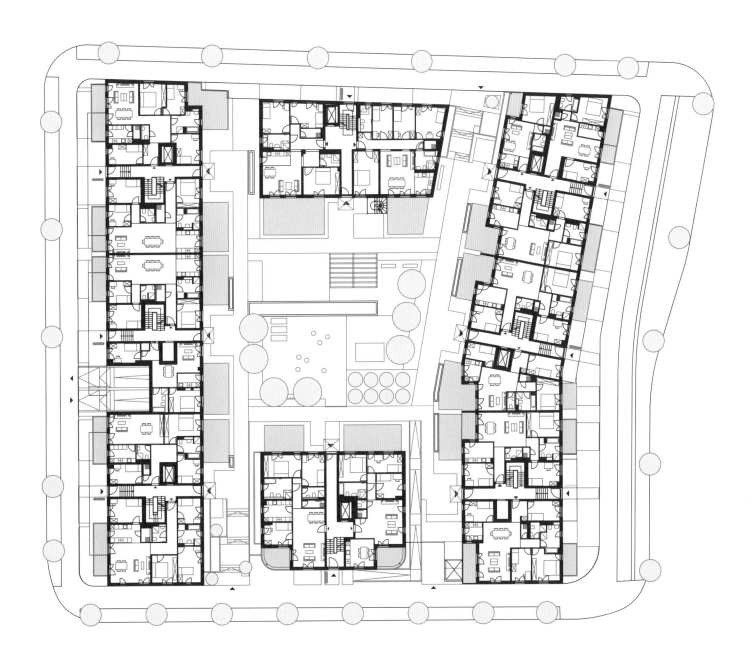

VENTILATION AND DENSITY
THE MODERN CITY BLOCK IS CHAR-
ACTERIZED BY HIGH URBANITY AND
DENSITY. THE OPEN GAPS AND THE
VARIED ALIGNMENT OF THE BUILD-
INGS CREATE AN AIRY INNER COURT-
YARD DESPITE THE LIMITED SPACE,
WHICH ENCOURAGES INTERACTION
AMONG RESIDENTS.

HANSATERRASSEN
BLAURAUM

LOCATION: WENDENSTRASSE 493/499, 20537 HAMBURG, GERMANY | **COMPLETION:** 2014 | **CLIENT:** HAMBURG TEAM PROJEKTENTWICKLUNGS GMBH | **LANDSCAPE ARCHITECTS:** WES & PARTNER LANDSCHAFTSARCHITEKTEN | **PHOTOGRAPHER:** WERNER HUTHMACHER

The design of individual buildings that are offset from each other gives all residents an unobstructed view of the water from the apartment and the balcony. The building heights are arranged in the urban development pattern in such a way that the common open terraces frame the construction complex. The new center of the quarter at the heart of the residential buildings contains a generously sized public square with playgrounds. Towards the river bank the construction deliberately retreats to preserve the public path network. The façade is divided into horizontal strips. The balustrade strips are made of white, slightly tinted plastering. To add depth to the façade, mosaic tiles made of ceramic glass were used in the window areas. The changing small tiles create an interplay of light that reflects the nearby canals. All living and dining rooms have a view of the water thanks to the precise design of the corners in the apartments. The balconies and railings are decorated with a QR code perforation, giving a lively look to the façade. The white-golden quarter contrasts with the neighboring clinker stone buildings, creating a signal for the transformation of the city district.

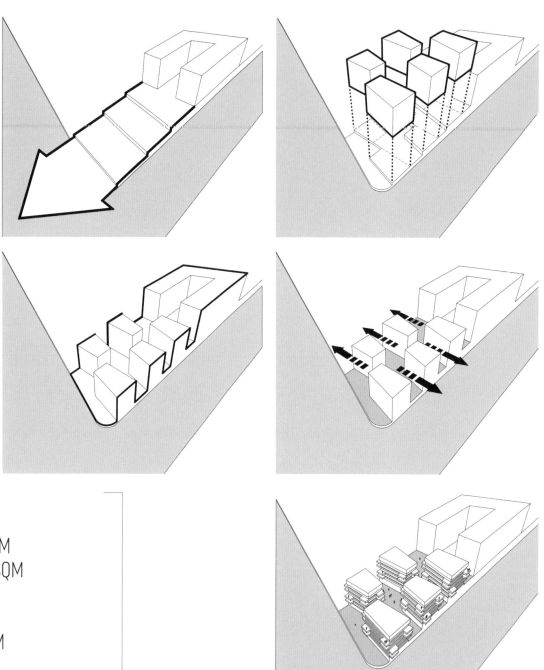

FACTS
SITE SIZE: 6,000 SQM
GFA TOTAL: 15,700 SQM
NO. BUILDINGS: 6
NO. UNITS: 131
ROAD LENGTH: 30 M
INHABITANTS: 400
KIND OF UNITS: 70-145 SQM
36 UNDERGROUND PARKING LOTS

The Hansaterrassen in the east of Hamburg border canal segments on both sides. The former industrial area remained unnoticed for a long time. The restructuring program of the city included the new construction of the districts in the eastern part of Hamburg that were severely damaged during World War II and reviving them by creating new residential areas. The new Hansaterrassen quarter is in the immediate vicinity of the historic Hansaburg, a building that was built in 1913–1915 by Lehmann & Hildebrandt and formerly used as a paper factory, parts of which are today listed. The quarter deliberately incorporates the urban planning conditions – for example, it replicates the typical Hamburg canal construction to create a uniform total ensemble in conjunction with the Hansaburg.

LIVING WITH A VIEW

THE RELATIONSHIP WITH THE WATER IS ESSENTIAL FOR THE HANSA-TERRASSEN PROJECT. THE DESIGN OF INDIVIDUAL BUILDINGS THAT ARE OFFSET FROM EACH OTHER GIVES ALL RESIDENTS AN UNOBSTRUCTED VIEW OF THE WATER FROM THE APARTMENT AND THE BALCONY.

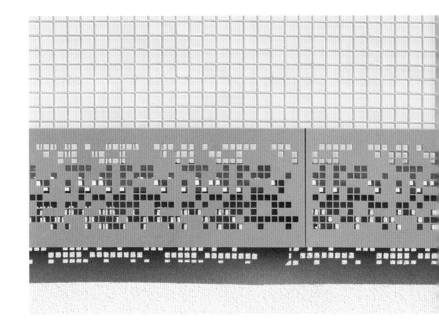

MOSAIK EILENRIEDE
MARAZZI + PAUL ARCHITECTS

LOCATION: MARS-LA-TOUR-STRASSE, 30655 HANOVER, GERMANY | **COMPLETION:** 2013 | **CLIENT:** HOCHTIEF SOLUTIONS, FORMART | **LANDSCAPE PLANNING COMPETITION:** KÖBER LANDSCHAFTSARCHITEKTUR | **LANDSCAPE DESIGN:** WIGGENHORN & VAN DEN HÖVEL | **PHOTOGRAPHER:** OLAF MAHLSTEDT, WETTBEWERBE AKTUELL

Similar to the urban development design of the quarter, the residential sheets are also fragmented. The front zones of the apartments are divided into private garden spaces while the remaining outdoor area constitutes a shared space. The parking spaces located in the basement section underneath the residential sheets are accessed from the periphery of the residential quarter. This way, the paths and squares located between the sheets remain car-free, increasing the quality of the locality for residents of the quarter and the immediate vicinity. The buildings on the residential sheets are accessed from the common space from which the residents have the option of directly reaching their private gardens on the ground floor. The design principle of grouping similar elements is repeated on the façades with the different variations of window shapes, wall openings, and plastered areas on the brickwork. However, the apartment layouts are quite different, not the least due to the ground plans that are not orthogonal.

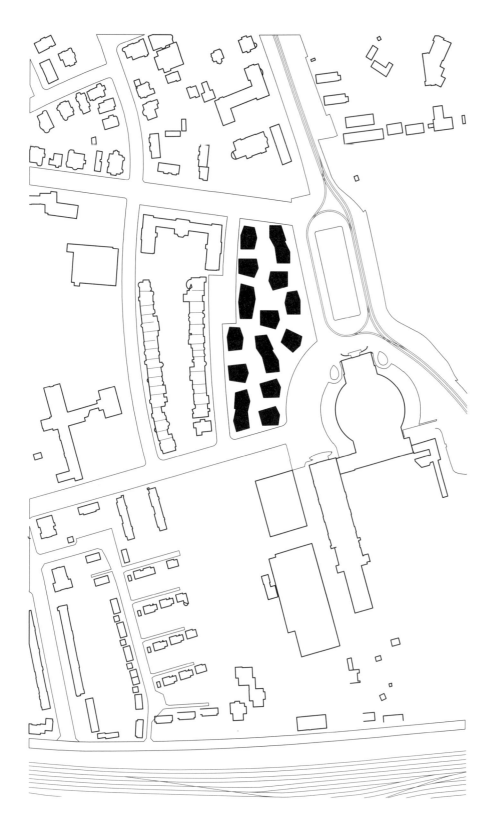

The premises on the Mars-La-Tour street are divided into differently sized sections, whose designs are reminiscent of sheets of floating ice. These residential sheets, on which two to four apartment houses are positioned, are raised and freely distributed across the building plot. This "drifting" creates interesting spatial constellations and interplay between spatial density and spaciousness. The paths that emerge between them meander like a river through the quarter. The inner banks constitute seating areas while the outer banks form the border to the private residential sheets. The paths expand into courtyards and squares that serve as recreational areas for the entire quarter and its vicinity, including the neighboring retirement home.

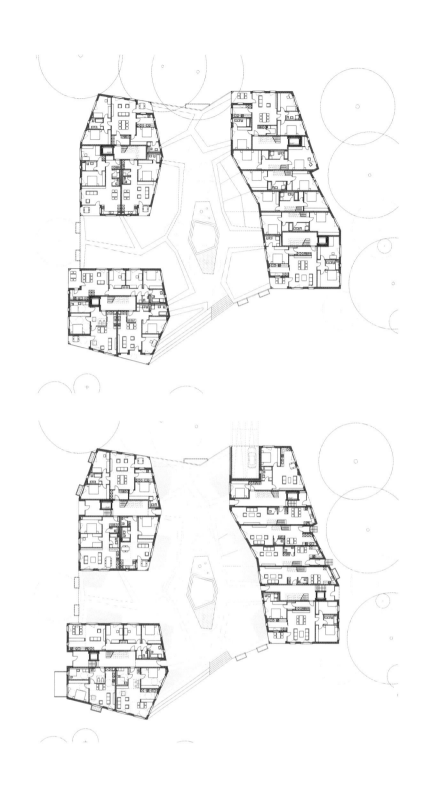

FACTS
SITE SIZE: 21,966 SQM
GFA TOTAL: 33,814 SQM
NO. BUILDINGS: 14
NO. UNITS: 162
ROAD LENGTH: 670 M
KIND OF UNITS: 1-4 BEDROOMS, 75-150 SQM
229 UNDERGROUND PARKING LOTS

URBAN DENSITY
THIS PROJECT SHOWS HOW, DESPITE HIGH URBAN DENSITY, HIGH-QUALITY CONSTRUCTION STRUCTURES WITH ATTRACTIVE OUTDOOR SPACES AND INTERACTION ZONES CAN BE CREATED.

PARK LINNÉ
KISTER SCHEITHAUER GROSS
ARCHITEKTEN UND STADTPLANER

LOCATION: EUPENER STR./HILDEGARD-VON-BINGEN-ALLÉE/CLARA-IMMERWAHR-WEG, 50933 COLOGNE, GERMANY | **COMPLETION:** 2017 | **CLIENT:** DORNIEDEN GENERALBAU GMBH | **COORDINATION:** IQ REAL ESTATE GMBH | **OPEN-AIR PLANT:** THORSTEN ZIETZ LANDSCHAFTS-ARCHITEKT | **PHOTOGRAPHER:** YOHAN ZERDOUN

Specially developed dyed concrete blocks and paving stones as well as water-bound floor covering reflect the desire to develop an urban whole. The PARK LINNÉ corner building COLÓN with its loggias responds to the presence of the tree branches with a grid of pilaster strips, creating a silent dialog of natural and architectural shapes through the interplay of shadow and sunshine. Yet the district square is a warm and welcoming place not only during the day, but in the evening as well with the specially developed illumination. The ensemble is framed by prominent high corner buildings that constitute the new edges of the quarter. The exteri-or of PARK LINNÉ is distinguished by clear shapes and harmonious façades. Various light-colored plastered sections alternate, giving the building a classical-modern look through receding and projecting sections. The front gates of the entrances are partially clad in natural stone slabs and give a visual structure to the entire ensemble. Floor-to-ceiling windows, loggias and roof terraces predominate. The entrances with doors based on the traditional home designs lead to staircases that give each villa a different character through the use of different colors, highlighting their individual touches.

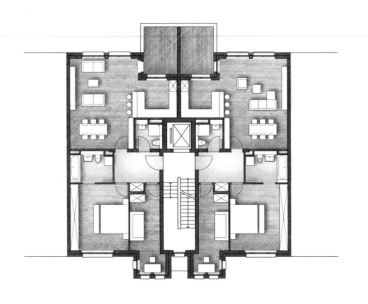

FACTS
SITE SIZE: 13,754 SQM
GFA TOTAL: 37,077 SQM
NO. BUILDINGS: 14
NO. UNITS: 203
ROAD LENGTH: 345 M
INHABITANTS: 600
KIND OF UNITS: 56-164 SQM
207 UNDERGROUND PARKING LOTS

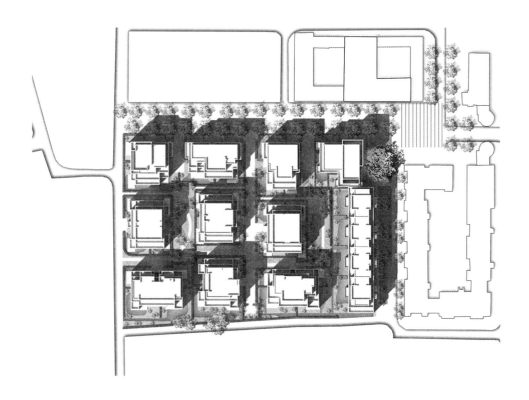

The Cologne districts Braunsfeld and Müngersdorf are among the most popular and coveted districts of the city due to their vicinity to the city park and the downtown area. They are dominated by elegant Wilhelminian villas and townhouses. Surrounded by nature in a nearly car-free district immediately neighboring the landmarked Sidol building of the former chemical factory, nine urban villas are under construction in addition to an already completed apartment building COLÓN in the PARK LINNÉ, which is a residential and landscape park.

The urban development concept is that of a city quarter with proportionate street areas, public squares and clearly identified separate houses in a public realm that reflects urbanity. Urban planning created a public square around the old sycamore tree that reminds every visitor and resident of the basic philosophy of handling traditions respectfully and their responsibility regarding sustainability.

HOMELY COLORS
WITH ITS LIGHT-COLORED FAÇADES AND INTRICATE ILLUMINATION SYSTEM, COLÓN IN PARK LINNÉ HAS A SIMULTANEOUSLY ELEGANT, WARM AND HOMELY ATMOSPHERE. THE STAIRCASES IN DIFFERENT COLORS SUPPORT THE IDENTIFICATION OF THE RESIDENTS WITH THE APARTMENT BUILDING.

BRICK NEIGHBOURHOOD
DEKLEVA GREGORIČ ARCHITECTS

LOCATION: ULICA IVANE KOBILCA 1-7, 1000 LJUBLJANA, SLOVENIA |
COMPLETION: 2014 | **CLIENT:** SSRS – NATIONAL HOUSING TRUST | **LAND-
SCAPE ARCHITECTURE:** DEKLEVA GREGORIČ ARCHITECTS, BRUTO D.O.O. |
PHOTOGRAPHER: MIRAN KAMBIČ

A clear systematic approach to the organization of 185 dwellings was developed to allow for an array of 17 different apartment types, varying in terms of size and internal arrangement to address the different needs of future residents. The position of the structure, installation and internal organization of the apartments with a backbone service strip allows internal flexibility – a diverse set of rooms distributed either as one large single space or a set of smaller rooms. The system allows the joining of smaller flats or separating of larger units, before, during and after construction. Connecting areas are naturally illuminated from two sides, thus the corridor becomes a meeting place.

Social interaction is upgraded by placing a shared common space above each building's entrance. This can be used for birthday parties, indoor playgrounds for wintery months, gym, or any other activity. Poems by Slovenian poets are printed on the glazing of the communal spaces. Each communal space of each residential community is thus enriched by the chosen poet. This contextual and semantic upgrade of the architecture allows the residents to identify even more with their living environment while at the same time enriching the cultural awareness of the inhabitants.

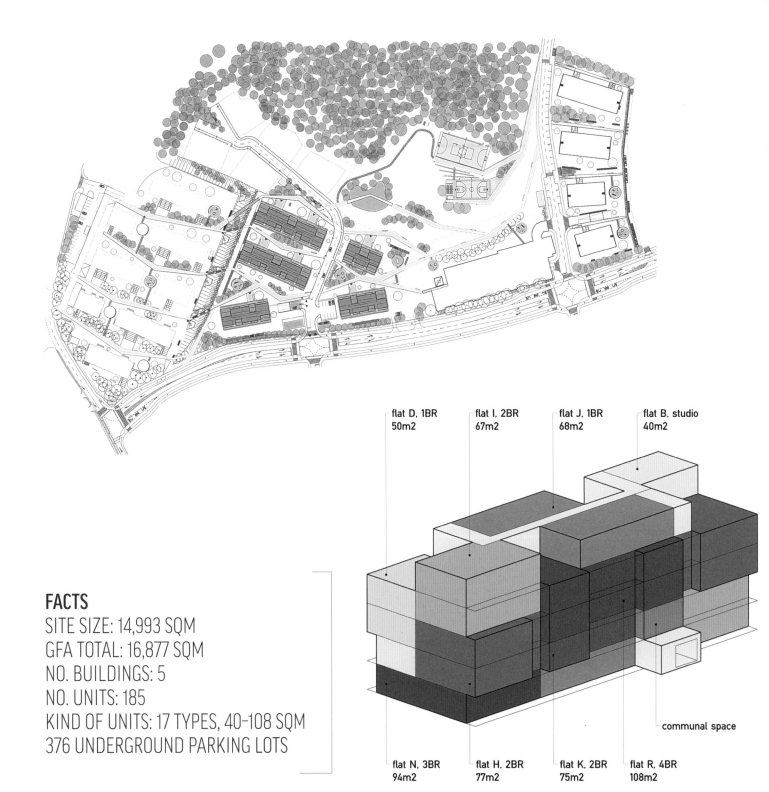

flat D, 1BR
50m2

flat I, 2BR
67m2

flat J, 1BR
68m2

flat B, studio
40m2

FACTS
SITE SIZE: 14,993 SQM
GFA TOTAL: 16,877 SQM
NO. BUILDINGS: 5
NO. UNITS: 185
KIND OF UNITS: 17 TYPES, 40-108 SQM
376 UNDERGROUND PARKING LOTS

communal space

flat N, 3BR
94m2

flat H, 2BR
77m2

flat K, 2BR
75m2

flat R, 4BR
108m2

How can a clear spatial, material and social identity be established in a neighborhood? This question was the basic principle when developing the design of structures and surroundings of this project to encourage a deeper connection of future residents with their living environment. The complex is located in the southwestern outskirts of the capital of Slovenia, Ljubljana, on the grounds of a former brick factory. The concept of 3D erosion results from a critique of the existing master plan with generic size and height volumes and their arbitrary position. This concept of sub-structuring of the volume is further reflected in the material expression: the initial envelope is defined as a brick layer, and the cut-outs with balconies are rendered.

LOCAL HISTORY

THE SELECTION OF BRICKS AS
A PRIMARY MATERIAL DERIVES
FROM THE MEMORY OF THE
FORMER BRICKYARD THAT WAS
LOCATED ON THE SITE. FURTHER-
MORE, BRICKS CAN BE USED AS
A MEANS OF EXPRESSION FOR
ADDITIONAL MICRO-STRUCTURING
OF THE FAÇADE SURFACE AND AC-
COMMODATE A UNIQUE IDENTITY.

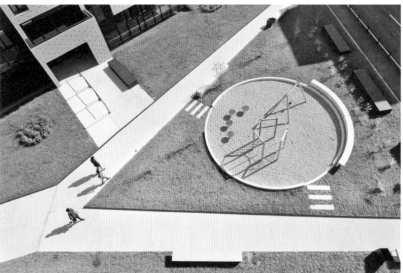

WOHNBEBAUUNG SEESIDE
BÄCHLEMEID

LOCATION: RUPPANERSTRASSE 14–14D, AESCHENWEG 3, 3A AND 3B, CONSTANCE,
GERMANY | **COMPLETION:** 2012 | **CLIENT:** DIH DEUTSCHE WOHNWERTE GMBH & CO. KG,
HKPE HOFKAMMER PROJEKTENTWICKLUNG GMBH | **LANDSCAPE DESIGN:** STÖTZER
LANDSCHAFTSARCHITEKTEN | **PHOTOGRAPHER:** ROLAND HALBE / ARTUR IMAGES

The existing developments extend along Ruppanerstraße, alternating between beautiful agricultural structures with farmyards facing the street and side-gabled main buildings situated right along the street. This interplay is taken up as a theme, developed and repeated. The residential concept is divided into seven farm-like structures. In line with their rural character they are arranged along a public stair system that extends along the slope, offering meeting points with fountains at various points. This creates a rural density with exterior and interior communication areas that are on a level with the terraces and gardens by intercepting them at split-level heights.

The buildings are developed with two and three-story envelopes. Entrances, foyers, public squares and the small terraces of the apartments aim to support interaction among the residents in addition to individual high-quality dwelling. Different apartment sizes of 65 to 150 square meters are developed across split levels to accommodate the slope. On the west and east side, the residences are designed with large terrace areas and views across Lake Constance. Next to the pedestrian paths, access is also provided from the underground garages.

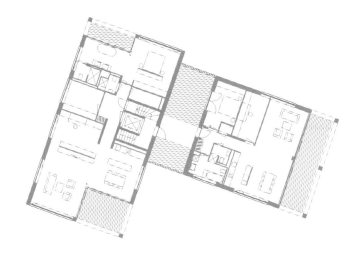

FACTS
SITE SIZE: 7,829 SQM
GFA TOTAL: 5,822 SQM
NO. BUILDINGS: 7
NO. UNITS: 50
ROAD LENGTH: 68.5 M
INHABITANTS: 100
KIND OF UNITS: 1–3 BEDROOMS
77 LOTS IN 2 UNDERGROUND PARKINGS

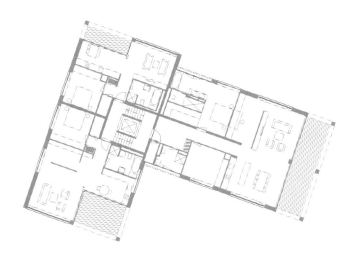

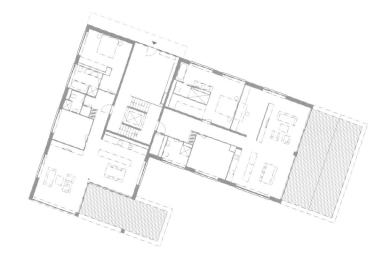

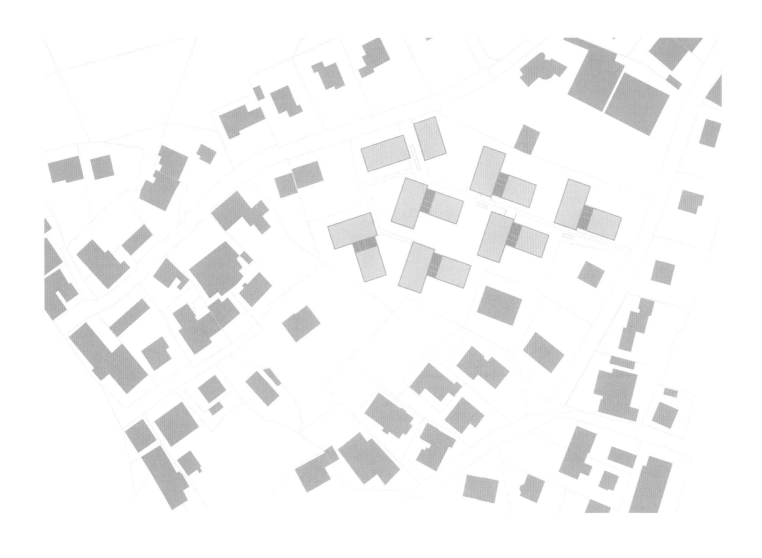

What makes this project unique is the high-quality treatment of the landscape and architecture. The Seeside residences emerged from an analysis of the location – on the one hand the delicate Lake Constance landscape and on the other the immediate vicinity to the historic city center of Constance-Allmannsdorf. The plot is distinguished by its situation on a slope and the view across Lake Constance, as well as the neighboring rural farm architecture and traditional orchards. In this setting, a cluster of seven, mostly orthogonal, farm-like structures was placed with layouts and positions that are offset to each other. The individual buildings extend along the slope, creating rural density, while their slight misalignment creates public squares with fountains, meeting areas, insights, and views. Towards the outside extend private areas with quiet orchards, offering views of the lake and the village center.

RURAL HARMONY
THE DELIBERATE RURAL DENSITY OF THE BUILDINGS IS IN HARMONY WITH THE LIGHTLY COLORED FAÇADES AND THE MODERN ARCHITECTURE LANGUAGE. GENEROUS LOGGIAS AND TERRACES OFFER PANORAMIC VIEWS. THE SURROUNDINGS ARE INCORPORATED IN THE INTERIOR DESIGN THROUGH OAK FLOORS, WARM ASHLAR SLABS AND ENVIRONMENT-FRIENDLY MATERIALS.

MYRICA
ARNOLD UND GLADISCH ARCHITEKTEN

LOCATION: SEBASTIANSTRASSE 21A, 10179 BERLIN, GERMANY | **COMPLETION:** 2014 | **CLIENT:** WOHNUNGSBAUGENOSSENSCHAFT "BEROLINA" EG | **PHOTOGRAPHER:** WERNER HUTHMACHER

This inner-city residential complex of five buildings with 95 residential units and a total living area of more than 8,400 square meters has been created on wasteland close to the former Berlin Wall. Generously proportioned loggias determine the rhythm of the buildings. The alternating smooth and graphically finely structured rendered surfaces emphasize the horizontal alignment of the buildings. Brick arches between the walls emphasize this impression on the head building of the ensemble. The available apartments ranging from two to five rooms address different target groups: singles, couples, and families with children to ensure a diverse structure of residents. In addition to classical layouts, the offers also include modern apartment solutions with open style kitchens, generous living/dining areas and variable individual rooms. Every apartment enjoys an attractive outdoor area in the form of a loggia or roof terrace. The vehicle traffic is served via a central underground garage that can be reached via elevator from four houses.

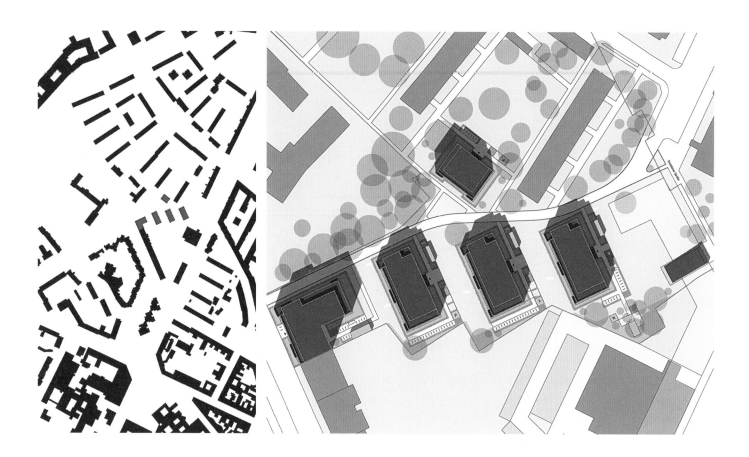

FACTS
SITE SIZE: 8,000 SQM
GFA TOTAL: 13,900 SQM
NO. BUILDINGS: 5
NO. UNITS: 95
ROAD LENGTH: 190 M
INHABITANTS: 240
KIND OF UNITS: 1-4 BEDROOMS, 39-133 SQM
40 UNDERGROUND PARKING LOTS

The project is located in the inner Berlin Mitte district. Its name is derived from the historic name of the later Luisenstadt, which covered parts of present Mitte and Kreuzberg districts. The building near Sebastianstraße is the highest of the five houses. With its emphasized corners it constitutes the urban development ending of the neighboring perimeter block and is also the head building of the new ensemble. A newly created path starts from this building and extends throughout the quarter based on the historic course of the former Alexandrinenstraße. The other new buildings are aligned along it. Their open line construction and the expansive greened areas link them to the neighboring existing buildings of the cooperative. The varying alignments and heights of the buildings and the variations of the façade theme resulted in individual building structures with a common exterior space with large areas of vegetation.

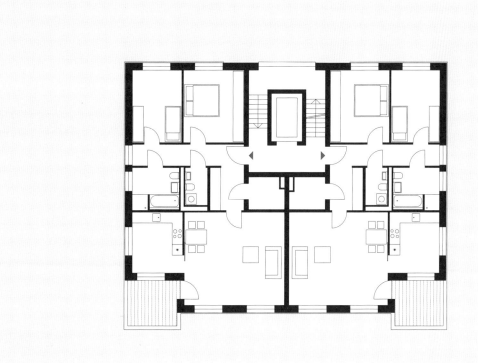

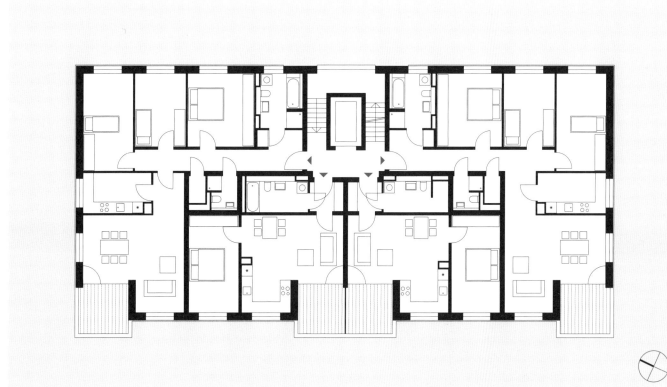

CONSTRUCTION WITH TRADITION
MYRICA HAS BEEN APPLYING THE TRADITION OF COOPERATIVE BUILDING SINCE THE 1920S. THE MATERIALS, STRUCTURES AND DETAILS OF THE COMPLEX REINTERPRET ELEMENTS OF THIS ERA IN A CONTEMPORARY WAY.

PARKSIDE ONE
KISTER SCHEITHAUER GROSS
ARCHITEKTEN UND STADTPLANER

LOCATION: RIA-THIELE-STRASSE 21-37, 40549 DUSSELDORF, GERMANY |
COMPLETION: 2014 | **CLIENT:** PANDION AG | **LANDSCAPE DESIGN:** EGL ENTWICKLUNG
UND GESTALTUNG VON LANDSCHAFT | **PHOTOGRAPHER:** YOHAN ZERDOUN

In the first construction stage of the Belsenpark project, ksg implemented parkside ONE, consisting of 85 condominiums with living areas ranging from 54 to 208 square meters. The three-to four-floor buildings with additional recessed top floors are grouped around a rectangular greened inner courtyard. To the north and the east the higher closed perimeter block development (four to five story high) screens the courtyard garden from the quarter's internal access road and the driveway into the shared underground garage. Towards the green belt of Belsenpark bordering on the south and towards the west, the lower urban villas are positioned as standalone structures to provide

views and access from the inner courtyard to the park. All two-, three-, four-, or five-room apartments are equipped with a terrace, a balcony or a garden. The stepped floors are especially generously proportioned with all-round terraces and floor plans of more than 140 square meters. The four- to five-story buildings were built in the massive construction style. The exterior walls are single-leaf constructions with a thermal insulation composite system and sand-line brickwork. The façade design of pure white with individual details such as the bay corners emphasized by decorative plates is based on the classical villa construction style of the district called Oberkassel.

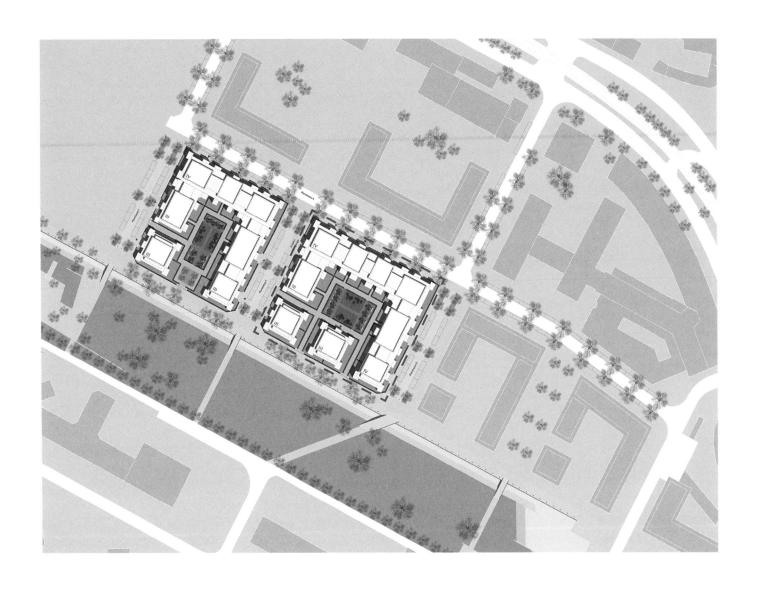

FACTS

SITE SIZE: 5,431 SQM
GFA TOTAL: 17,000 SQM
NO. BUILDINGS: 3
NO. UNITS: 85
ROAD LENGTH: 235 M
INHABITANTS: 215
KIND OF UNITS: 54–208 SQM
86 UNDERGROUND LOTS

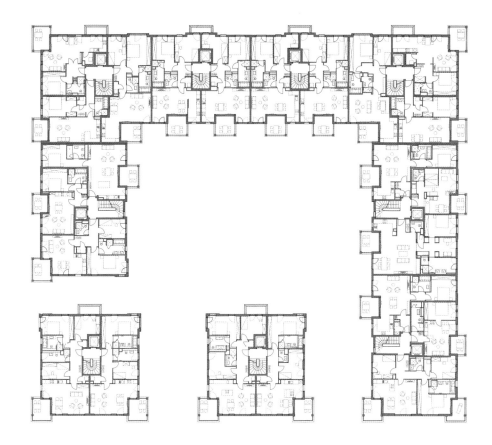

Parkside ONE is located on the 15.2 hectare premises of a former freight terminal on the left bank of the Rhine in Oberkassel, one of Dusseldorf's most attractive districts. Since the abandonment of the terminal, the premises are among the city key urban development projects. The city required a sustainable, integrative and green project and all involved parties, citizens, neighbors, as well as politics and business representatives, were involved in the planning process from the outset. Ten

percent of the total area is dedicated to plants and water and the residential area is intercepted by several green axes. The overall concept accommodates all central aspects of life: dwelling, working, living and relaxing.

DISTINGUISHED DESIGN
THE URBAN AND ELEGANT QUARTER IS HARMONIOUSLY EMBEDDED IN THE SURROUNDING VILLA DISTRICT AS WELL AS THE NEIGHBORING PARK LANDSCAPE. IT IS DISTINGUISHED BY ELABORATE ENTRANCE DESIGNS AND THE STRUCTURE AND PROPORTIONS OF CLEAR GEOMETRICAL SHAPES THAT EMBELLISH THE PURE WHITE FAÇADES.

GANEI SHAPIRA - AFFORDABLE HOUSING
ORIT MUHLBAUER EYAL ARCHITECTS

LOCATION: ARYE DE MODENA STREET 17, TEL AVIV, ISRAEL | **COMPLETION:** 2014 | **CLIENT:** TEL AVIV MUNICIPALITY | **LANDSCAPE ARCHITECT:** TAL ROSEMAN | **PHOTOGRAPHER:** SHAI EPSTEIN

The project encompasses 69 apartments, which are available for rent under the affordable housing scheme. They include 42 3-bedroom apartments (around 80 square meters) and 27 4–5-bedroom apartments (90–120 square meters).

In planning the project, a special emphasis was given to the open communal spaces and to the green spaces of the neighborhood. Several planning alternatives for the project were examined. The chosen plan had the highest potential to allow the community to evolve as a real collegial neighborhood, in the spirit of old times, a kind of an "urban kibbutz". The center of the project is the communal space in the middle, which also serves as a passage through the project to the park and as the entrance area to the buildings. It also functions as a natural continuation to and from the green spaces through which the residents can reach the De Modina Garden. The architectural design is a modern interpretation of the "Shikun" residential housing projects that were built during the years of the massive immigration to Israel (1950–1960). However, unlike the old neighborhoods, Ganei Shapira offers high building standards.

The Ganei Shapira project was built on a 4,050-square-meter plot, owned by the Tel Aviv municipality. It is located between Tueri Zahav Street and De Modina Street of the Shapira neighborhood. The Tel Aviv municipality provided a substantial plot for the benefit of the community for this truly unique project. This made the Shapira neighborhood attractive to middle class families and serves as a valid and compelling response by the authorities to the demands of the middle class of the "Rothschild protest" of 2011/2012, which had been caused by massive rent increases, among other reasons.

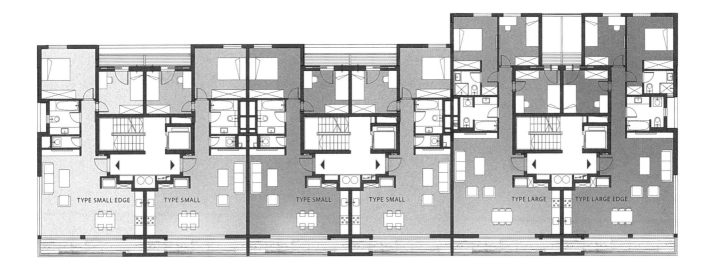

TYPE SMALL EDGE   TYPE SMALL   TYPE SMALL   TYPE SMALL   TYPE LARGE   TYPE LARGE EDGE

FACTS

SITE SIZE: 4,046 SQM
GFA TOTAL: 10,500 SQM
NO. BUILDINGS: 3
NO. UNITS: 69
ROAD LENGTH: 60 M
INHABITANTS: 250
KIND OF UNITS: 42× 3 BEDROOMS
(80 SQM), 27× 4-5 BEDROOMS
(90-120 SQM)
70 UNDERGROUND PARKING LOTS

LIVING COMMUNITY
IN A NEIGHBORHOOD WHERE RENTAL
FEES ARE NEARLY NO LONGER AF-
FORDABLE, GANEI SHAPIRA OFFERS
AFFORDABLE LIVING SPACE WITHIN
AN ESTABLISHED COMMUNITY.

WOHNQUARTIER STERNENHOF
MORE ARCHITEKTEN

LOCATION: SESSENHEIMER STRASSE 2-8, 79110 FREIBURG IM BREISGAU, GERMANY |
COMPLETION: 2014 | **CLIENT:** FREIBURGER STADTBAU GMBH | **OPEN SPACE PLANNING:**
CHRISTINE BOSCH | **PHOTOGRAPHER:** YOHAN ZERDOUN

The commissioning of one out of three construction projects resulted from a second place contest entry of the year 2009. A large array of accommodations was created within the four buildings ranging from two-room apartments to barrier-free three- and four-room apartments up to five-room penthouse-apartments with roof patios. The different typologies of the row houses arranged in triples and the point houses arranged in doubles with staircases located inside alternate between solitaires and quadrangles. Whilst the cubature creates spatial variations and clear separate identities, they are all combined by the universal treatment of the façades. The recesses of the attic floors of all buildings take adjacent free spaces into account. The fronts are a play of varying degrees of insulation thickness and the granularity of the finishing coat. Smooth areas with glossy surfaces around the windows alternate with light roll-on plaster structures. This alternation is repeated on a larger scale between the front and sides of the buildings. This resulted in individual buildings, which can also be seen as a large cohesive ensemble and with the help of color distinct exterior, interim and front zones.

FACTS

SITE SIZE: 3,550 SQM
GFA TOTAL: 5,814 SQM
NO. BUILDINGS: 4
NO. UNITS: 44
ROAD LENGTH: 25.5 M
INHABITANTS: 110
KIND OF UNITS: 1-4 BEDROOMS
48 UNDERGROUND PARKING LOTS

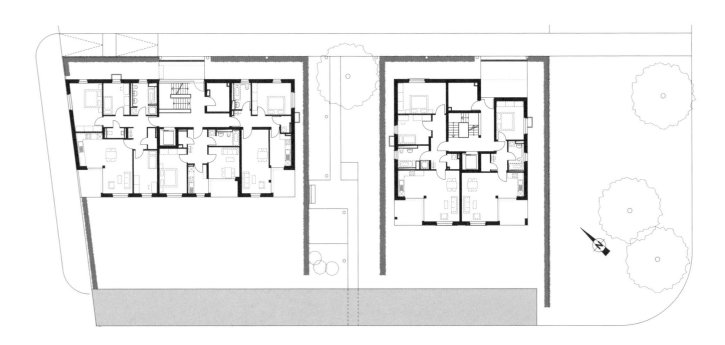

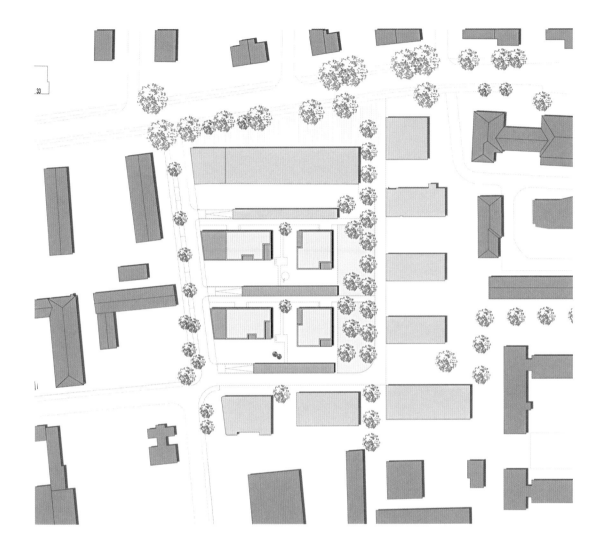

The four buildings are part of the residential complex Wohnquartier Sternenhof, which consists of twelve buildings overall. They constitute an independent ensemble within the quarter through the use of common design elements. One row of apartments and a point house each are paired in a cooperative unit with an underground garage. A green stretch runs along the eastern border of the plot, the core of the urban development, while on the western side the row buildings border the public street. A ground upturn marks the border between public and private open spaces. Private access ways on the northern side of the buildings connect entryways and peripheral structures, creating a passage between both public areas. The ground floor apartments have private gardens that face south.

ROOM SEQUENCES
THE VARIOUS COLORED FRONT WALLS OF THE BUILDINGS CREATE SEPARATE ROOM SEQUENCES. THE COLORS OF THE FRONT WALLS REEMERGE ON THE RECESSED EDGING. CHANGES IN THE SURFACE STRUCTURE CREATE A HIGH-QUALITY APPEARANCE WITH ECONOMIC MEANS.

CHILESTIEG
BAUMSCHLAGER EBERLE

LOCATION: GLATTTALSTRASSE, RÜMLANG, SWITZERLAND | **COMPLETION:** 2014 | **CLIENT:** IMMOBILIEN COMPAGNONI AG ZURICH | **LANDSCAPE DESIGN:** SCHWEINGRUBER ZULAUF LANDSCHAFTSARCHITEKTEN | **PHOTOGRAPHER:** EDUARD HUEBER, ARCH PHOTO, INC.

The hexagonal layout of the buildings and the shimmering façade give the apartment buildings, totaling 1,600 square meters of constructed space, a striking look. The building edges take the streets and surrounding buildings into account. The rear-ventilated façade is made of a three-millimeter thick hot-dip galvanized steel sheet. The metal façade surface renders the edges and corners of the buildings precisely and clearly discernible, additionally highlighting the hexagonal building shape. The metal surface catches and reflects the light and the surrounding green, underscoring the impression of the highly polished structures.

The grid of jointing of the steel sheets was kept as large as possible and matched to the window opening formats. On a total useful space of 4,300 square meters, the three apartment buildings contain 41 apartments with three to five rooms each. Most apartments face south and west. To maximize daylight, each apartment has room-high loggia windows in the living area. The ground floor apartments have gardens as private outdoor spaces.

FACTS
SITE SIZE: 6,500 SQM
GFA TOTAL: 6,200 SQM
NO. BUILDINGS: 3
NO. UNITS: 41
ROAD LENGTH: 106 M
INHABITANTS: 125
KIND OF UNITS: 2-4 BEDROOMS
43 UNDERGROUND PARKING LOTS
AND 3 VISITOR PARKING LOTS
ON THE SITE

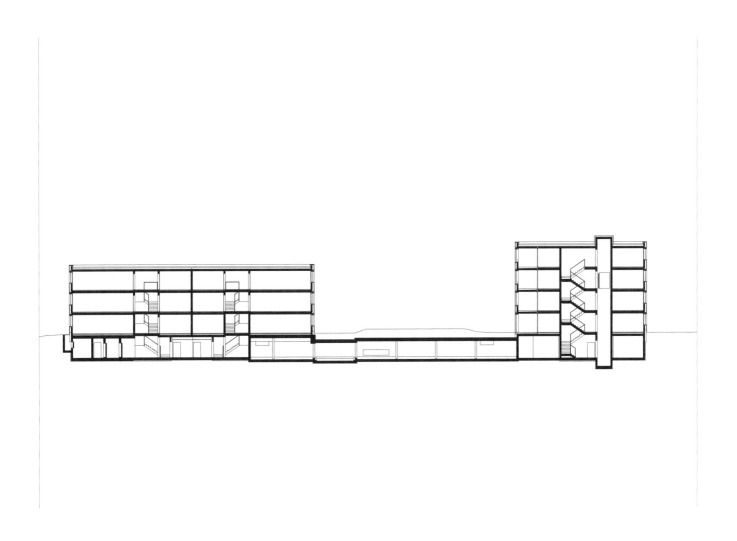

The Chilestieg development is located in the Rümlang community north of Zurich. The plot and construction of Chilestieg is framed by a green belt of tall expansive trees. Measuring 6,500 square meters, the premises are bordered to the north by Chilestieg and in the east by the Glatttalstrasse. baumschlager eberle planned a loosely structured residential development that sensitively integrates the structure and nature of the surroundings. The location and alignment of the three- to four-story buildings is based on the surrounding volumes. The buildings keep a distance from each other and their loose positioning emphasizes the park-like nature of the complex. Between them and the trees on the borders of the property, hedges with various thicknesses and flowering shrubs naturally provide borders among public and semi-public spaces and private zones.

LANDSCAPE INTEGRATION

WITH THEIR SHAPE AND THE REFLEC-
TIVE COVER OF GALVANIZED STEEL
SHEETS, THE APARTMENT BLOCKS RE-
SEMBLE SHIMMERING CRYSTALS IN A
GARDEN. YET THEY ARE NOT FOREIGN
BODIES, BUT RATHER OBJECTS FROM
A CHAMBER OF WONDERS THAT
REFLECT THE NATURE SURROUNDING
THEM.

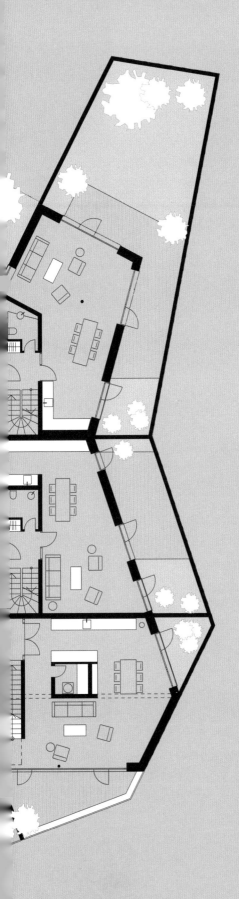

SINGLE-FAMILY HOUSING
DEVELOPMENTS

BLUE POOL ROAD
RONALD LU & PARTNERS

LOCATION: 11–39 BLUE POOL ROAD, HAPPY VALLEY, HONG KONG, CHINA |
COMPLETION: 2013 | **CLIENT:** LOCKOO LIMITED (HANG LUNG PROPERTIES LIMITED) |
EXTERIOR DESIGN ARCHITECT: KOHN PEDERSEN FOX | **PHOTOGRAPHER:** RONALD LU &
PARTNERS

11–39 Blue Pool Road development involves nine 3-story luxury semi-detached houses, a 2-story utility building, a guardhouse, and two retaining walls at the front and back of the houses along Blue Pool Road in Hong Kong. Situated in a densely built urban area, this development provides approximately 60 percent of open area with hard-paved landscape and planting, including vertical green walls, planters and water features for the enjoyment of the residents. The major façade design of the houses was inspired by traditional Chinese folding elements. Double-glazed units with integrated solar-sensed blinds and high-performance low-emissivity coating were applied, which optimize energy efficiency, enhance the level of solar control to the internal space, and reduce undesirable glare both inside and outside. The rest of the external walls were provided with insulation to reduce heat gain inside the houses. The development places a high priority on the environment. The whole development is in line with the strategy of reducing, recycling, reusing and renewing throughout the construction and design process. Different from most of the residential projects in Hong Kong, the American US Green Building Councils LEED certification for Homes International Pilot Scheme assessed the building performance of the nine houses, and the project achieved a gold rating.

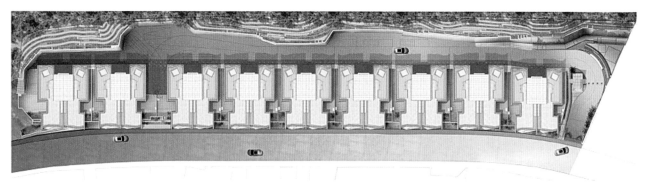

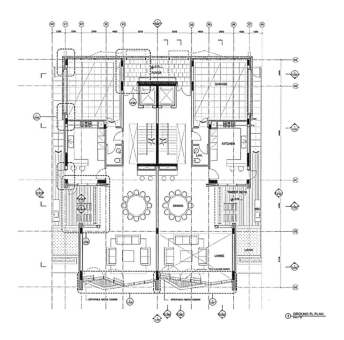

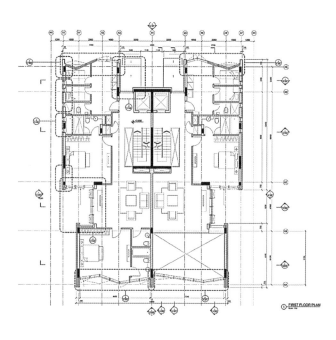

The development of 11–39 Blue Pool Road places a high priority on the environment. Sustainability was emphasized by the choice of materials, the water recycling system, energy efficient appliances and lighting systems, and the enhancement of the landscape quality. Through the sustainable design, which is suitable for Hong Kong's urban context and sub-tropical climate, an environmentally responsible lifestyle has been provided for the future residents and surrounding neighbors.

This development can serve as a reference model for the upcoming green building development in the region.

FACTS

SITE SIZE: 7,850 SQM
GFA TOTAL: 8,585 SQM
NO. BUILDINGS: 9
NO. UNITS: 9
ROAD LENGTH: 200 M
KIND OF UNITS: SEMI-DETACHED
HOUSES
36 PARKING LOTS IN 18 INDIVIDUAL
GARAGES

TRADITION

THE MAJOR FAÇADE DESIGN OF
THE HOUSES WAS INSPIRED BY
TRADITIONAL CHINESE FOLDING
ELEMENTS.

LEBEN AM OBSTHAIN
JOSEF WEICHENBERGER
ARCHITECTS + PARTNER

LOCATION: PELARGONIENWEG, 1220 VIENNA, AUSTRIA | **COMPLETION:** 2009 | **CLIENT:** HEIMBAU GEMEINNÜTZIGE BAU-, WOHNUNGS- UND SIEDLUNGSGENOSSENSCHAFT, REG. GMBH | **LANDSCAPE DESIGN:** AUBÖCK+KÁRÁSZ LANDSCHAFTSARCHITEKTEN | **PHOTOGRAPHER:** LISA RASTL

A landscape with a special identity was created on the outskirts of Vienna. The construction of the garden complex Leben am Obsthain (Life at the Orchard) plays with the gentle hills, while various combinations of the two basic house styles add variety and incorporate a large amount of nature. The ground floor of the different house types contains open, yet roofed car parking spots and this transparent design creates a connection between the street and garden landscape. The 61 single-family homes have minimum construction depths, thus light and sun highlight the living areas. On the interior there are no constructional bearing structures, an ideal basis for customized finishing from a loft apartment to a multi-bedroom apartment. Some of the roof areas are accessible and can be used as vegetable gardens or roof terraces. The gardens and common green areas were not fenced to facilitate flowing transitions. The grouping of the buildings is also suitable for multi-generation and large family dwellings.

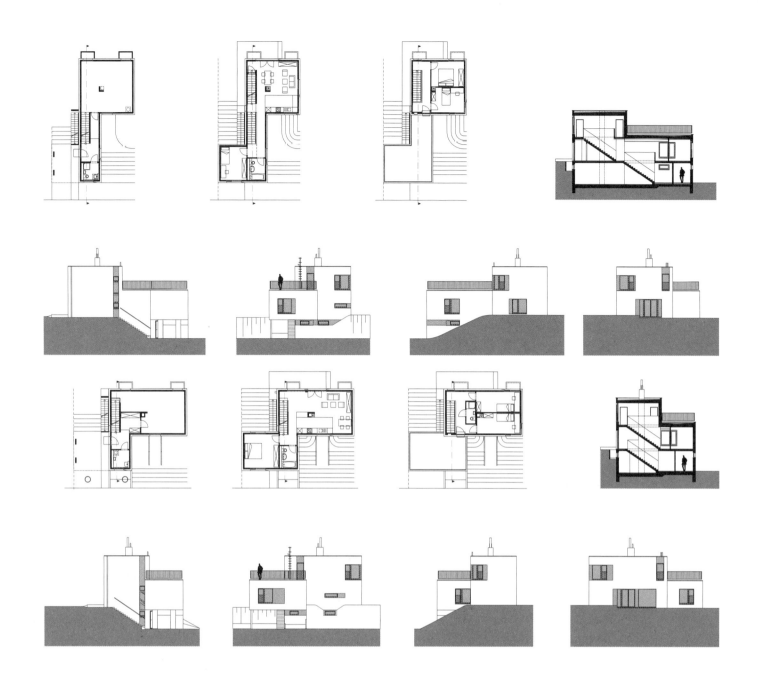

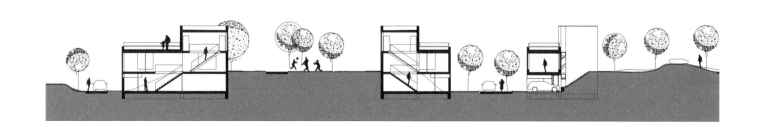

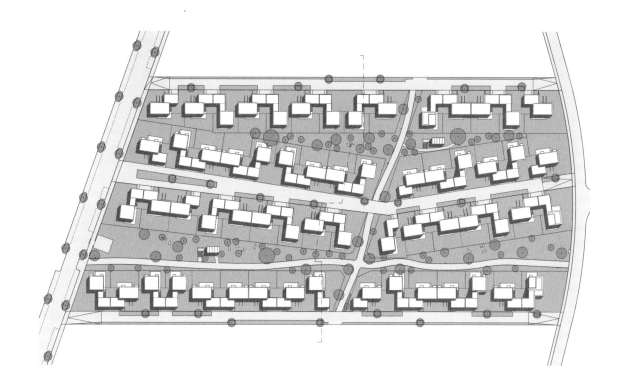

FACTS
SITE SIZE: 23,582 SQM
GFA TOTAL: 11,600 SQM
NO. BUILDINGS: 61
NO. UNITS: 61
ROAD LENGTH: 750 M
INHABITANTS: 200
KIND OF UNITS: DETACHED HOUSES
61 CAR PORTS
COMMUNITY GREENHOUSES AND
FRUIT CELLARS

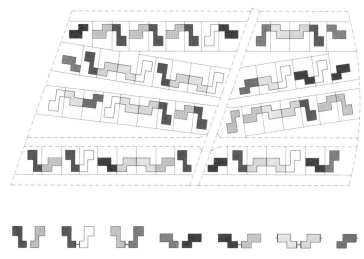

The complex in the 22nd district on the border of Vienna is located inside a large traditional orchard. It is embedded in gentle hills and an orchard of apple, pear, cherry and walnut trees. The complex is bordered to the north and south by streets and the west and east by agricultural areas. A school, kindergarten, pharmacy, post office and local suppliers as well as a swimming lake and sports ground are in the vicinity. The construction is dominated by loose structures and many interim spaces, mostly consisting of the common green spaces of the fruit orchards. To add more character to the landscape, the terrain was gently shaped into dunes. Community greenhouses and old fruit storage cellars provide space for workshops and events. All passing streets are traffic reduced and pedestrian paths cross the entire complex.

CAREFUL IMPLEMENTATION
THE SINGLE-FAMILY HOMES WERE
EMBEDDED IN A SPATIAL SEQUENCE
OF GENTLE HILLS AND GROUND
INDENTATIONS IN THE MIDDLE OF A
FRUIT AND NUT ORCHARD, COMPLE-
MENTED BY SHARED SPACES SUCH AS
GREENHOUSES AND FRUIT CELLARS.

TOWNHOUSES ST. LEONHARDS GARTEN
AHAD ARCHITEKTEN

LOCATION: SANKT-LEONHARDS-GARTEN, BRUNSWICK, GERMANY | **COMPLETION:** 2011 | **CLIENT:** BAUGRUPPE UPPER EASTSIDE | **PHOTOGRAPHER:** ADRIAN SCHULZ

The new quarter offers families a viable alternative to living in the periphery of the city. The entire quarter was constructed by owners' collectives and this specific element was designed for three families. Despite the common construction grid and standardized building elements, the structured volumes were developed in a way that created private terraces and roof gardens. The different types of bricks and a small gap on the face clearly distinguish the aligned buildings from each other. Seen from the garden, however, the group is covered by a homogenous plaster surface, giving the impression of a single structure with many protrusions and recesses, terraces and vertical as well as horizontal window fronts. On the inside, the buildings also follow the bright and open tradition of Classical Modernity. Three basic layouts were used to create individual homes – a small house for two, a compact house for a large family, and a home with an office. The courtyard is used as a shared play and recreation area.

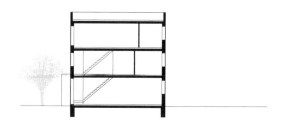

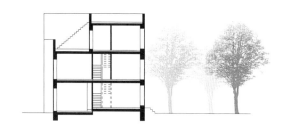

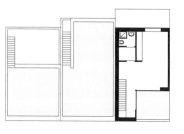

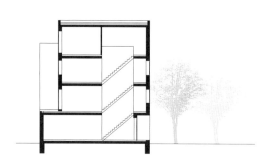

FACTS
SITE SIZE: 510 SQM
GFA TOTAL: 630 SQM
NO. BUILDINGS: 3
NO. UNITS: 3
ROAD LENGTH: 18 M
INHABITANTS: 6-15
KIND OF UNITS: 125-185 SQM
1-2 PARKING LOTS PER UNIT
OFFICE ON GROUND FLOOR OF HOUSE 16

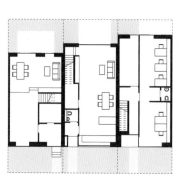

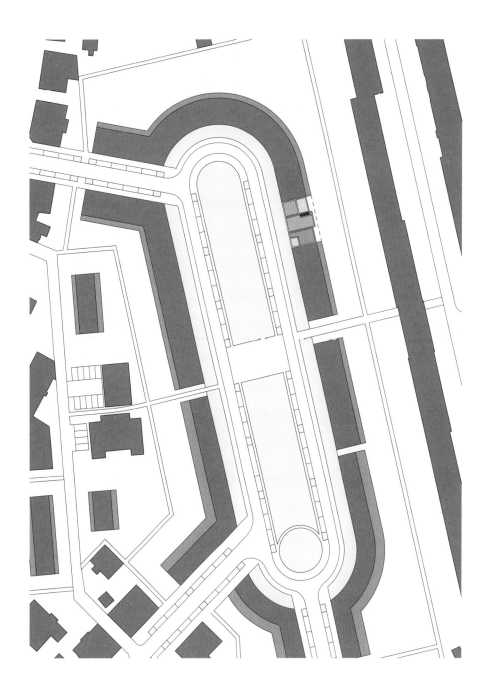

Offering a valuable area in a central location, the premises of the former streetcar depot were the base for the development of a residential quarter with very special features. The urban development design was contributed by Klaus Theo Brenner of Berlin. It involved multi-story townhouses as well as apartments in city villas to ensure a mixed population structure in the quarter. In front of the buildings there is a five-meter-wide area followed by a six-meter-wide reduced traffic section. At the heart of the quarter there is a 19-meter-wide and 160-meter-long square that extends from north to south. A competition of several stages determined the prerequisites for the materials and overall elevation, and specified the implementation of the buildings in groups as construction units.

OWNER'S COLLECTIVE
THE ENTIRE QUARTER WAS
SUPPORTED BY THE FEDERAL
DEPARTMENT OF TRANSPORT,
BUILDING, AND HOUSING AS AN
EXPERIMENTAL RESIDENTIAL
AND URBAN DEVELOPMENT
PROJECT OF THE RESEARCH AREA
OF INNOVATIONS FOR FAMILY
AND SENIOR CITIZEN-FRIENDLY
CITY QUARTERS.

LAS ANACUAS INCREMENTAL HOUSING
ELEMENTAL

LOCATION: PRADOS DE SANTA CATARINA, MONTERREY, MEXICO | **COMPLETION:** 2009 |
CLIENT: INSTITUTO DE VIVIENDA DE NUEVA LEÓN | **PHOTOGRAPHER:** RAMIRO
RAMIREZ

Building incremental housing is not a choice, it is a constraint. In the best of cases, governments and markets are able to build houses of forty square meters. Instead of reducing the size, however, the builders of Las Anacuas countered scarcity with the principle of increment housing, focusing on what is more difficult and what cannot be done individually by people themselves, and what will guarantee the common good in the future. In Monterrey the houses underneath and duplex apartments on top have an initial cost of $20,000. They can be enlarged to up to seventy-two square meters, which equals the floor area of a middle-income standard house. The design was based on the concept of low-rise high density, without over-crowding, with the possibility of expansion – from social housing to middle-class dwelling. The families are expected to benefit from that added value and from the fact that the cost of land facilitates the availability of services and opportunities.

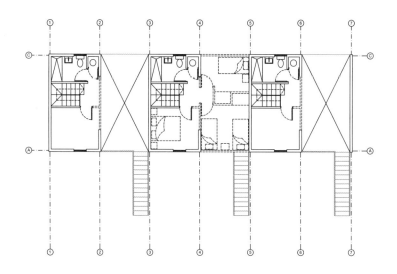

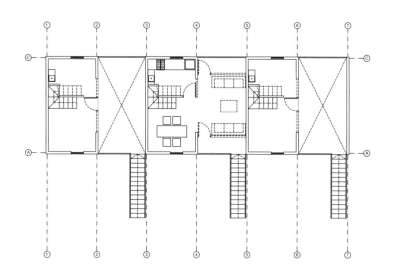

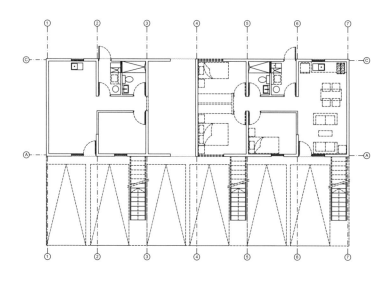

FACTS
SITE SIZE: 6,591 SQM
GFA TOTAL: 2,957 SQM
NO. BUILDINGS: 70
NO. UNITS: 70
INHABITANTS: 280
KIND OF UNITS: INCREMENTAL HOUSING
84 PARKING LOTS

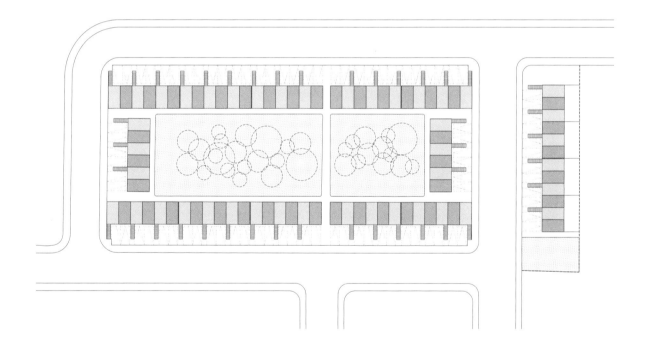

The project is located in Monterrey, the capital of the northern Mexican state Nuevo León, the second wealthiest city in Mexico and an important place of business. On the Mexican housing market it is difficult to find a house for less than $30,000. Therefore the economically disadvantaged cannot be properly served. Also, the necessity to consider sustainability and environmental protection in housing has been increasing considerably in recent times. In Santa Catarina, a municipal district of Monterrey where the average cost for a house is $50,000, the Institute for Housing ventured a step to solve those issues by building Las Anacuas.

ADAPTABILITY
THE AFFORDABLE HOUSES AND DUPLEX APARTMENTS OF LAS ANACUAS RESPOND TO THE CHANGING NEEDS OF THEIR RESIDENTS IN THE COURSE OF TIME. THE FLOOR AREAS CAN BE EXPANDED WITH GROWING NEEDS FOR MORE SPACE.

XIXI WETLAND ESTATE
DAVID CHIPPERFIELD ARCHITECTS

LOCATION: 21 ZIJINGANG ROAD, HANGZHOU, CHINA | **COMPLETION:** 2015 | **CLIENT:** HANGZHOU WESTBROOK INVESTMENT CO. LTD. | **LANDSCAPE ARCHITECTS:** BELT & COLLINS | **PHOTOGRAPHER:** SIMON MENGES

The apartment buildings of Xixi Wetland Estate by David Chipperfield Architects are surrounded by a water garden, which, as a reference to the wetland park, is a mostly wild landscape. In contrast to these green surroundings, the twenty-two-story apartment buildings are dark stone volumes embedded in the water garden. Although their skin has the appearance of solid masonry, the eight-centimeter-thick basalt bricks are suspended from the structure and elastically jointed to comply with seismic requirements. 21-centimeter-high horizontal concrete bands, which are made in situ, sandblasted, articulate the façades and color stainds. The buildings are placed on a concrete plinth that sits in the water. This plinth forms the base of a village group with various levels, walls, and balustrades creating a sequence of exterior spaces that provide access to the buildings. The interiors are characterized by floating spaces. Room-high windows let in natural light and offer views across the water garden.

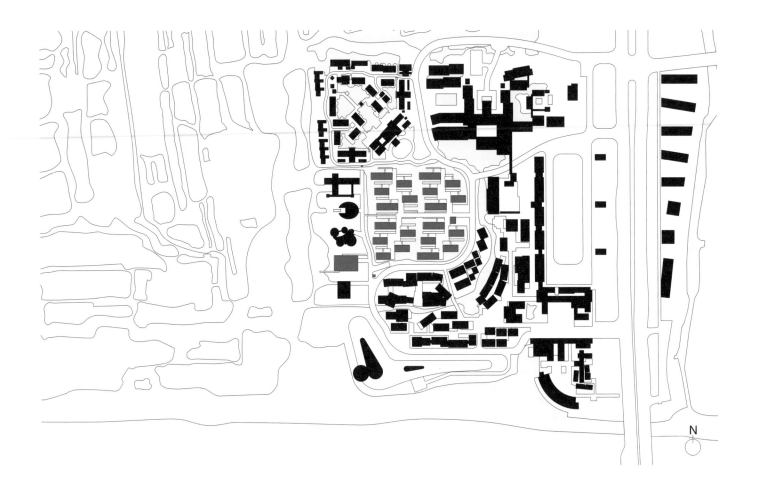

FACTS
SITE SIZE: 40,700 SQM
GFA TOTAL: 11,800 SQM
NO. BUILDINGS: 20
NO. UNITS: 40
KIND OF UNITS: 2-3 BEDROOMS
90 UNDERGROUND PARKING LOTS

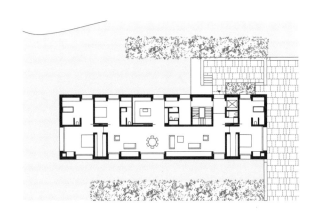

Xixi is a national wetland park located on the outskirts of Hangzhou, the capital of Zhejiang Province in eastern China. Situated at the head of Hangzhou Bay, where the Grand Canal meets the East China Sea, Xixi is a natural area that has been shaped by humans for over a thousand years. Water is the distinctive and formative feature of the park that is densely crisscrossed by six main watercourses as well as various ponds, lakes and swamps. The omnipresent relationship between landscape, architecture, and water is key to the atmosphere in Xixi. Capturing and integrating this atmosphere was the main goal of the design of the new apartment buildings. In contrast, the strictly north-south orientation of the buildings underlines the estate as a fabricated structure within the wilderness.

ATMOSPHERE

THE OMNIPRESENT RELATIONSHIP BETWEEN LANDSCAPE, ARCHITECTURE, AND WATER DEFINES THE ATMOSPHERE IN XIXI, WHICH HAS ALSO BEEN CONSIDERED DURING THE DEVELOPMENT PROCESS OF THE NEW APART-MENT BUILDINGS.

LIVING PLACES SUBURBAN REVIVAL
BENT ARCHITECTURE

LOCATION: DANDENONG, VICTORIA, AUSTRALIA | **COMPLETION:** 2012 | **CLIENT:**
DEPARTMENT OF HEALTH AND HUMAN SERVICES | **PHOTOGRAPHER:** TREVOR MEIN

Initiated by the Office of the Victorian Government Architect and the Office of Housing, Living Places Suburban Revival involves the design of fifteen environmentally efficient, low-cost dwellings on six consolidated residential allotments in Dandenong, a southeastern suburb of Melbourne. The project is spatially diverse and accommodates numerous household configurations. Double-story components are located on the northern side of the dwellings to ensure direct solar access into neighboring private open spaces. Private open spaces, semi-private gardens and operable fences and screens allow residents to mediate contact with neighbors, while centrally located communal outdoor spaces – one for passive recreation and outdoor spaces – one for passive recreation and one for active play – activate the site and create possibilities for interaction and self-expression. The project establishes a solar responsive urban framework, which, in combination with efficient internal planning and the integration of ecologically sustainable development technologies, facilitates dwellings with energy ratings in excess of eight stars. Water-sensitive urban design principles, gray water treatment, and indigenous planting reduce the site's dependence on public water and minimize its impact on the local environment.

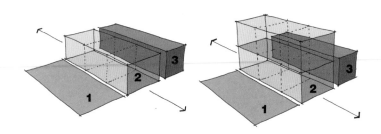

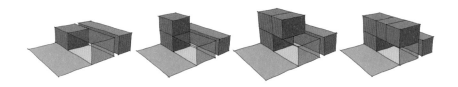

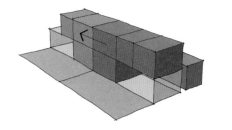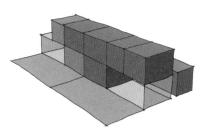

FACTS
SITE SIZE: 3,129 SQM
GFA TOTAL: 1,348 SQM
NO. BUILDINGS: 9
NO. UNITS: 15
ROAD LENGTH: 84 M
INHABITANTS: 38
KIND OF UNITS: DETACHED AND
SEMI-DETACHED TOWNHOUSES
15 PARKING LOTS

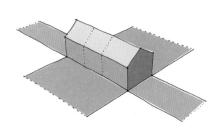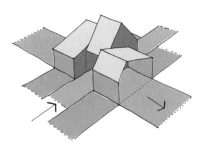

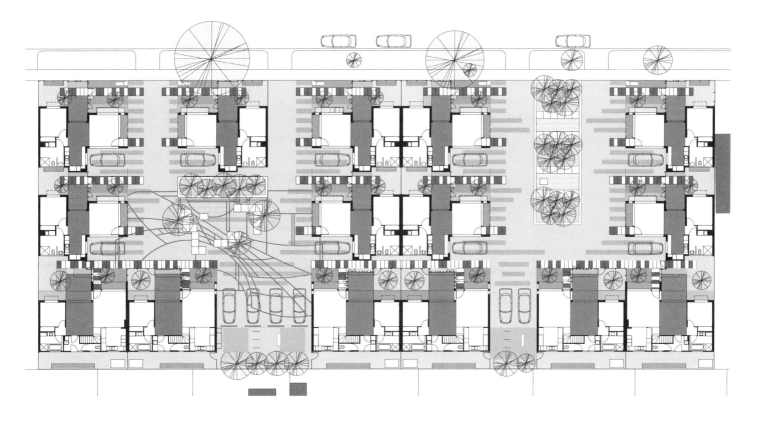

Living Places Suburban Revival is the culmination of an open design competition to establish an innovative approach to medium density public housing that can sensitively integrate with and rejuvenate low-density suburbs in an environmentally and socially sustainable way. The project offers a variety of household configurations that allow the development to respond to shifting demographics. Housing bands, landscape zones, pathways, and communal open spaces are overlaid. Private open spaces employ devices such as operable fences and screens, allowing residents to mediate their contact with the site community and neighborhood at large.

SUSTAINABILITY
LIVING PLACES SUBURBAN RE-VIVAL ESTABLISHES A SOLAR RESPONSIVE URBAN FRAMEWORK FOR THE DESIGN OF ENERGY-EFFI-CIENT DWELLINGS THAT RESPOND POSITIVELY TO THEIR SUBURBAN CONTEXT.

WOHNEN AM STROM
MICHELS ARCHITEKTURBÜRO

LOCATION: HOHE STRASSE, 51149 COLOGNE, GERMANY | **COMPLETION:** ONGOING |
CLIENT: CONFIDENTIAL | **VISUALIZATION:** MICHELS ARCHITEKTURBÜRO

The concept stipulates dense construction on the building lot with a very diverse structure of two- to three-story garden yard types. Without any spectacular effects, the different dimensions and concise buildings create an appropriate presence that evolves naturally from the functions and structures. The ground floor access to all residential units, in part from the public streets via protective front yards, in part via an internal alley and a small central square, accommodates individuality as well as casual social contacts. Inside the houses, there are attractive room situations with relations to the outdoor. Both the protected garden courts that extend the ground-floor living areas to the outdoors in various ways, as well as

the generous roof terraces with views of the river landscape of the Rhine promise high living and dwelling quality. The layouts are generously structured and designed. The focus was on providing a reasonable range of different apartment sizes. The intertwined and variously designed single-family homes are surprisingly generously proportioned despite the high density, coupled with a unique interlacing of protectiveness and openness.

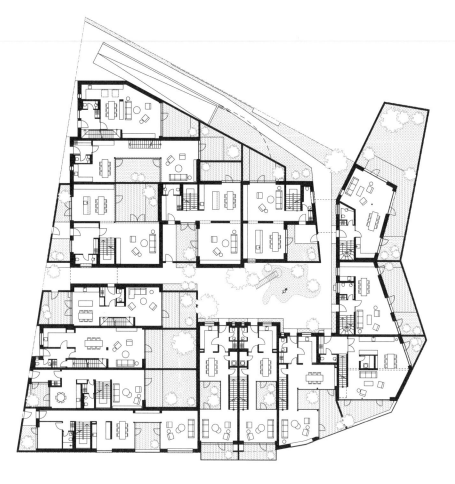

FACTS
SITE SIZE: 3,190 SQM
GFA TOTAL: 4,400 SQM
NO. BUILDINGS: 13
NO. UNITS: 13
ROAD LENGTH: 55 M
INHABITANTS: 50
KIND OF UNITS: SINGLE-FAMILY
HOUSES
18 PARKING LOTS FOR RESIDENTS
IN UNDERGROUND PARKING

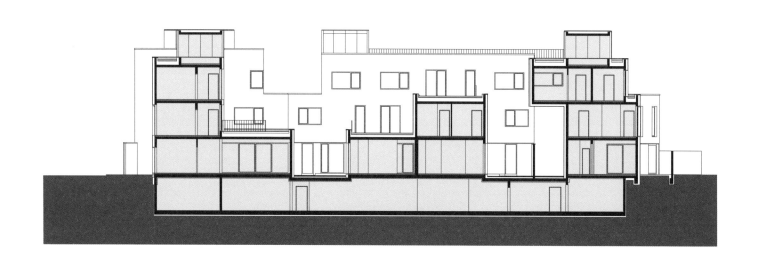

Wohnen am Strom on the right bank of the Rhine in Cologne is based on the idea of reproducing the historical density of old villages near the Rhine with their interweaving small alleys and their heterogeneous structure – locations that are distinguished by their compact buildings coupled with moderate height differences. The result is a building ensemble with surprisingly varied dwelling qualities, which, despite its relative high density is integrated into the rural context. The project is intended as an innovative contribution to the topic of condensed living quarters within the context of transformation of former rural structures in the vicinity of large cities. It is also naturally linked to the riverside landscape. Height gradation that is planned in detail provides views of the Rhine from every residential unit.

TRANSFORMATION
DESPITE ITS HIGH DENSITY, THIS
INNOVATIVE CONTRIBUTION TO
CONDENSED LIVING WITHIN THE
CONTEXT OF TRANSFORMATION
OF FORMER RURAL STRUCTURES
IN THE VICINITY OF LARGE CITIES
HAS SUCCEEDED IN ALLOCATING
INDIVIDUAL OUTDOOR AREAS
AND UNIQUE VIEWS OF THE
RHINE TO EACH RESIDENTIAL UNIT.

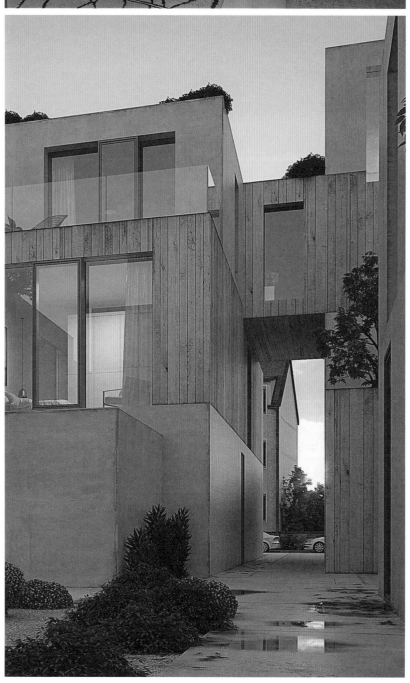

SAN DAMIAN HOUSING ESTATE
CHAURIYE STÄGER ARQUITECTOS

LOCATION: CAMINO SAN FRANCISCO DE ASÍS, LAS CONDES, CHILE |
COMPLETION: 2014 | **CLIENT:** CONFIDENTIAL | **PHOTOGRAPHER:** PABLO BLANCO

The San Damian Housing Estate project's first design strategy relies on two basic house models. The second floors of those models are rotated alternately so as to obtain six unique houses. The second strategy consists in making a clear distinction between the ground floor, jigsaw-like and irregular, and the second floor, rectangular and linear. This vertical differentiation provides covered spaces on the ground floor, which can in turn be used as access ways and balconies. This way the project offers the prospect of community ties through two main operations: on the one hand, by moving the parking underground, which helps to improve public space above ground, and on the other hand by creating a central space surrounded by six distinctive houses, which confers a sense of identity and variety to the estate. The housing complex is characterized by its clarity of forms and its clean façades in plain white. A sophisticated lighting design along the pedestrian corridors of the common area helps to create a pleasant atmosphere, inviting the neighbors to meet outside.

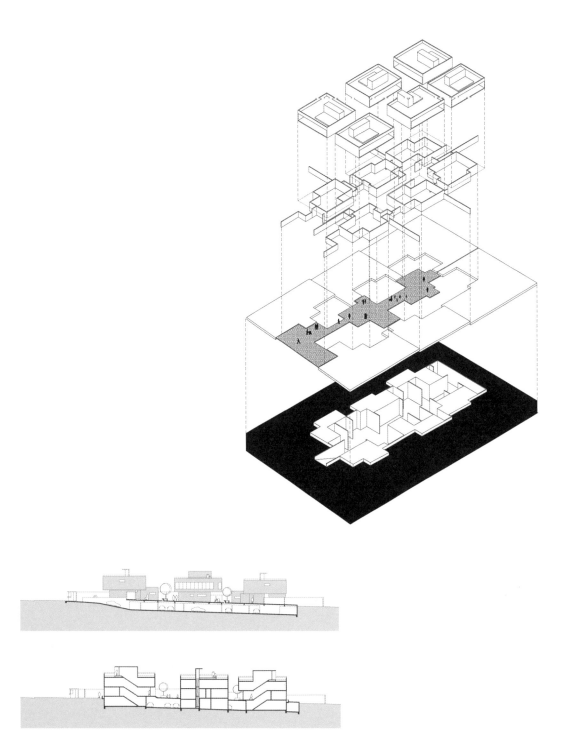

This project is set in the easternmost part of Santiago, in Las Condes, a rapidly developing pre-Andean district populated by the country's economic elite. Growth here has tended to rely on terraced housing schemes. In contrast with the community-based approach, this type of housing attempts to replicate the model of the semi-detached house but reproduces the same prototype as many times as it takes to fill the site, to such a degree that communal areas are reduced to bare parking lots. In the San Damian Housing Estate project Chauriye Stäger Arquitectos adopt another course. The residents of the estate are granted their privacy, but can at the same time develop a community live.

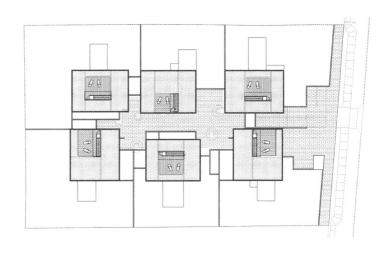

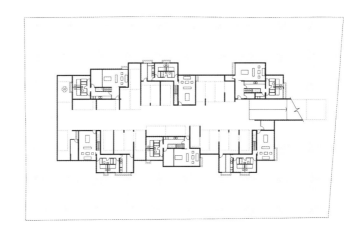

FACTS
SITE SIZE: 4,500 SQM
GFA TOTAL: 3,200 SQM
NO. BUILDINGS: 1
NO. UNITS: 6
ROAD LENGTH: 45 M
KIND OF UNITS: TOWNHOUSES
27 UNDERGROUND PARKING LOTS

NEIGHBORS' MEETING PLACE
THE MAIN OBJECTIVE OF THE PROJECT IS TO CREATE A CENTRAL SPACE OF COMMON USE, MOVING THE PRIVATE PARKING LOTS UNDERGROUND, PROVIDING PEDESTRIAN ACCESS TO EACH HOUSE.

NEWHALL BE
ALISON BROOKS ARCHITECTS

LOCATION: HARLOW, ESSEX CM17 9FA, ENGLAND | **COMPLETION:** 2012 | **CLIENT:**
LINDEN HOMES & GALLIFORD TRY | **PHOTOGRAPHER:** PAUL RIDDLE

This 84-unit scheme for Linden Homes completes phase 1 of the award-winning Newhall development in Harlow, Essex. Alison Brooks Architects' approach integrates a mix of new and established house typologies, prefabricated timber construction, and a highly efficient master plan to maximize living space and flexibility of the individual homes. The scheme's geometric and material consistency was inspired by the powerful roof forms and simple materials of Essex's rural buildings. The architects utilized these geometries to bring light into terraced courtyard houses, allow rooms in the attic, allow oblique views to the landscape beyond the site, and to introduce a sculptural rhythm to the scheme's streetscapes. The development con-

sists of four building types: five apartment buildings containing six, seven or eight apartments each; 14 villas; 29 courtyard houses, and seven townhouses, 26 percent of which are economically priced. All have covered front porches, central stair halls, roof terraces, Juliette balconies, and cathedral ceilings. Loft spaces either are finished as bedrooms or can be retrofitted as workspaces, additional bedrooms, or games rooms. Villas and courtyard houses have a ground floor study. This street-facing office space allows residents to take advantage of electronic media and 21st century home working lifestyles, helping to transform a residential suburb into an economically active community.

Sir Frederick Gibberd's 1949 vision for Harlow New Town was a series of neighborhoods of 6,000–10,000 people with a number of public facilities at its center. These are separated by "green wedges" and connected to the town center by public transport and cycle corridors. Newhall is a new neighborhood within that structure; a community of 6,000 people with a central public square and mixed use core. The landowners manage the development. Newhall Be is located in the south-western corner as one of the gateways to the development. Alison Brooks Architects' site plan enhances this master plan structure with a denser block pattern generated by their back-to-back courtyard house typologies. Apartment buildings mark the thresholds to the neighborhood, creating an urban edge in a suburban context.

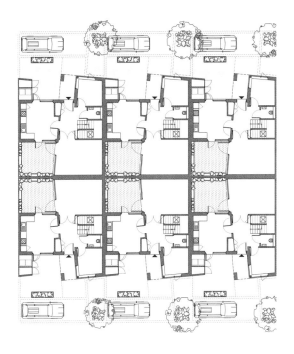

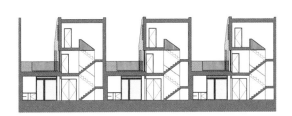

FACTS

SITE SIZE: 1,620 SQM

GFA TOTAL: 8,200 SQM

NO. BUILDINGS: 55

NO. UNITS: 84

ROAD LENGTH: 690 M

INHABITANTS: 370

KIND OF UNITS: 14 DETACHED HOUSES,
29 BACK-TO-BACK / COURTYARD HOUSES,
7 TERRACED HOUSES

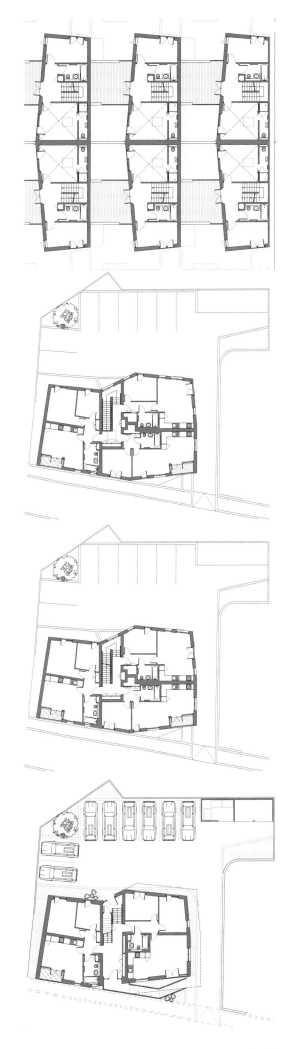

TERRACED HOUSES METAMORPHOSE
THE COURTYARD HOUSES ARE A
RADICAL CONVERSION OF TYPICAL
LONG AND NARROW 5 × 20 METER
TERRACED HOUSE PLOTS TO 9.5 × 10.5
METER PLOTS. THIS ALLOWS A VERY
WIDE HOUSE FOOTPRINT, T-SHAPED
WITH COURTYARD SPACES OR "OUT-
DOOR ROOMS" THAT INTERLOCK WITH
KITCHEN/DINING AND LIVING ROOMS.

VILLA VERDE INCREMENTAL HOUSING
ELEMENTAL

LOCATION: RÍO MAULE, CONSTITUCIÓN, CHILE | **COMPLETION:** 2013 | **CLIENT:** ARAUCO | PLAN DE VIVIENDA PARA TRABAJADORES | **FURTHER PARTICIPANTS:** PHILIP ZURMAN, PATRICIO BERTHOLET, FERNANDO MONTOYA | **PHOTOGRAPHER:** ELEMENTAL

The Arauco Forest Company was looking for a plan to support their employees and contractors in gaining home ownership, within the context of Chilean housing policies. Given the greater availability of resources, instead of taking one of the cheaper housing units and delivering it almost ready-to-use, the architects applied the principle of incremental construction, with an initial and final growth scenario of higher standards. The initial area of each unit is 55 square meters, however, it can be enlarged to up to 85 square meters. The architects used a participatory design process and included the families in the process of understanding constraints and priorities. Thus, ELEMENTAL was responsible for identifying the design conditions that belong to the "hard half" of the house and built precisely what was relevant to the family that they would not be able to build by themselves. The builders provided the frame, and from then on, families took over. They are still expanding their houses to this day, from social housing to middle-class units.

FACTS
SITE SIZE: 85,362 SQM
GFA TOTAL: 30,000 SQM
NO. BUILDINGS: 484
NO. UNITS: 484
INHABITANTS: ABOUT 1,936
KIND OF UNITS: INCREMENTAL HOUSING
200 PARKING LOTS
3 ADDITIONAL BUILDINGS

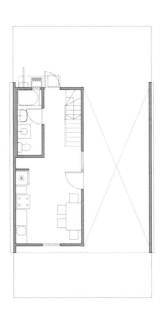

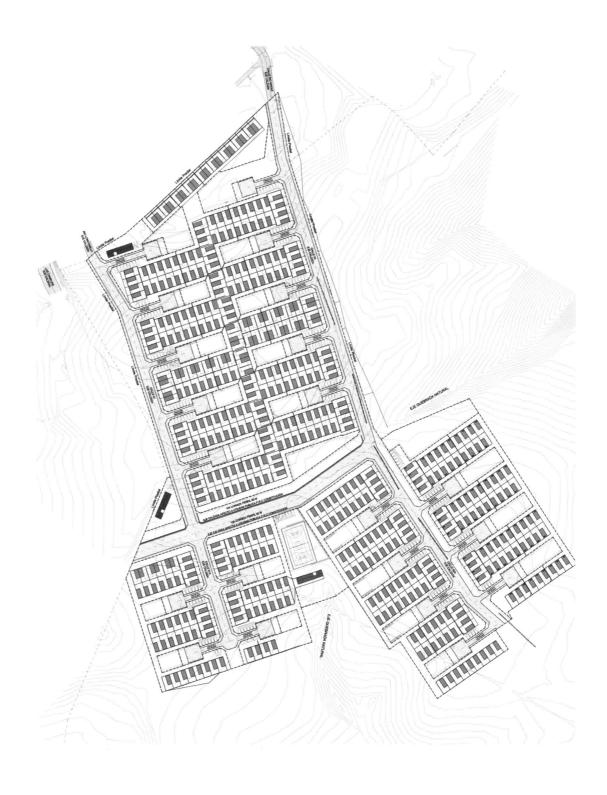

In 2010, an earthquake of 8.8 magnitude hit Chile. The country withstood the earthquake, but not the tsunami that came with it. Almost 500 people died and a large part of the infrastructure was destroyed. After the natural catastrophe, the architectural office ELEMENTAL was given 100 days to come up with a strategy for rebuilding the city of Constitución, formerly populated by 45,000 and located 400 kilometers south of Santiago, which had been almost completely destroyed. Villa Verde Incremental Housing is situated near the pacific coast along a street named after the river Río Maule which ends at the Pacific Ocean in the north of Constitución.

PARTICIPATORY DESIGN
THE RESIDENTS OF VILLA VERDE ARE ABLE TO ACTIVELY INFLU-ENCE THE BUILDING PROCESS AND TO DESIGN THEIR HOUSES ACCORDING TO THEIR NEEDS AND WISHES. THE FLOOR AREA OF EACH HOUSING UNIT CAN BE EX-PANDED BY 30 SQUARE METERS.

VICEM BODRUM RESIDENCES
EAA EMRE AROLAT ARCHITECTURE

LOCATION: ATATÜRK CAD. 184, BODRUM MUĞLA, TURKEY | **COMPLETION:** 2014 |
CLIENT: VICEM YACHTS | **PHOTOGRAPHER:** CEMAL EMDEN (152 M. AND B.),
THOMAS MAYER

The Vicem Residences are located on a rocky untouched protruding strip of land near Bodrum, Turkey. The development scheme is an experiment of mass fragmentation focusing on the stereotypical "large single house" that is predominant in the region. The topography was treated three dimensionally with a focus on functional relationships and attractive views. The buildings were designed to integrate with the natural surroundings and even to seemingly dissolve into the rocky site, as the surfaces of the ground-level structures were given a look as natural as possible. Thick stone walls provide efficient isolation and keep the interior cool in summer and warm in winter. The structures that are located above the ground floor level have a light, evanescent design. Their façades are covered in wooden louvers that can be adjusted to the position of the sun. The façades of the lower buildings can be opened completely, allowing them to merge and appear as a single space. With the help of cross-ventilation, shady courtyards in-between the buildings provide a cool breeze on hot summer days.

FACTS
SITE SIZE: 13,200 SQM
GFA TOTAL: 12,970 SQM
NO. BUILDINGS: 21
NO. UNITS: 21
ROAD LENGTH: 150 M
KIND OF UNITS: 7 LAYOUTS, 275-380 SQM
30 PARKING LOTS

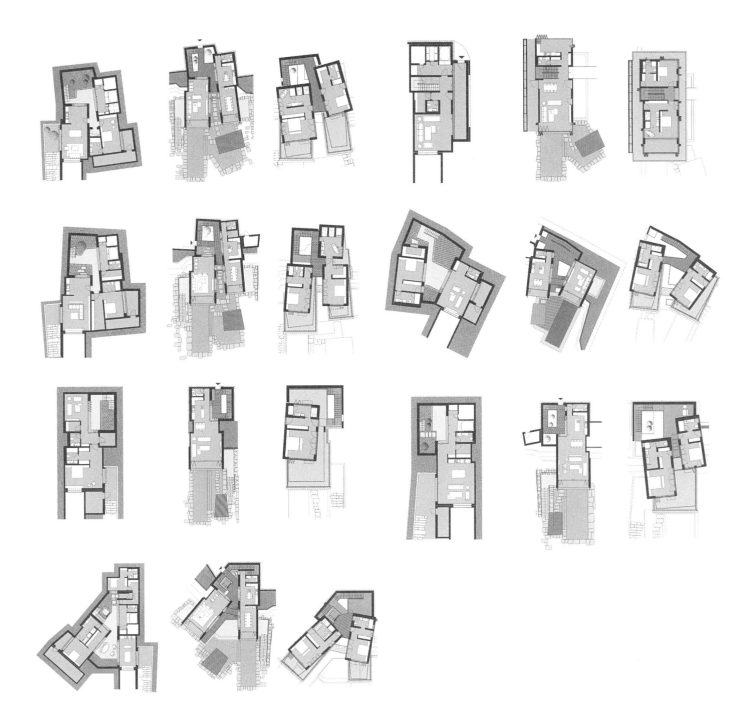

Located on the strip of land between the sea and the coastal road from Bodrum to İçmeler, one of Turkey's most popular holiday destinations, the group of buildings is unobtrusive. The nature of the landscape was preserved, providing surprising freshness in contrast with the density of buildings inside Bodrum. The landscape was designed simi-larly. Instead of heavily planted over-green areas, it is inspired by the different surface characters of the rocky texture and various bushes of the exist-ing natural landscape.

UNTOUCHED NATURE
THE TENSION THAT ARISES FROM THE CONFLICT OF THE VIRGIN QUALITY OF THE COAST AND THE DENSE PHYSICAL PATTERN THAT WAS BUILT ON THE SITE EMERGED AS THE MOST CRUCIAL DRIVER FOR THE DESIGN.

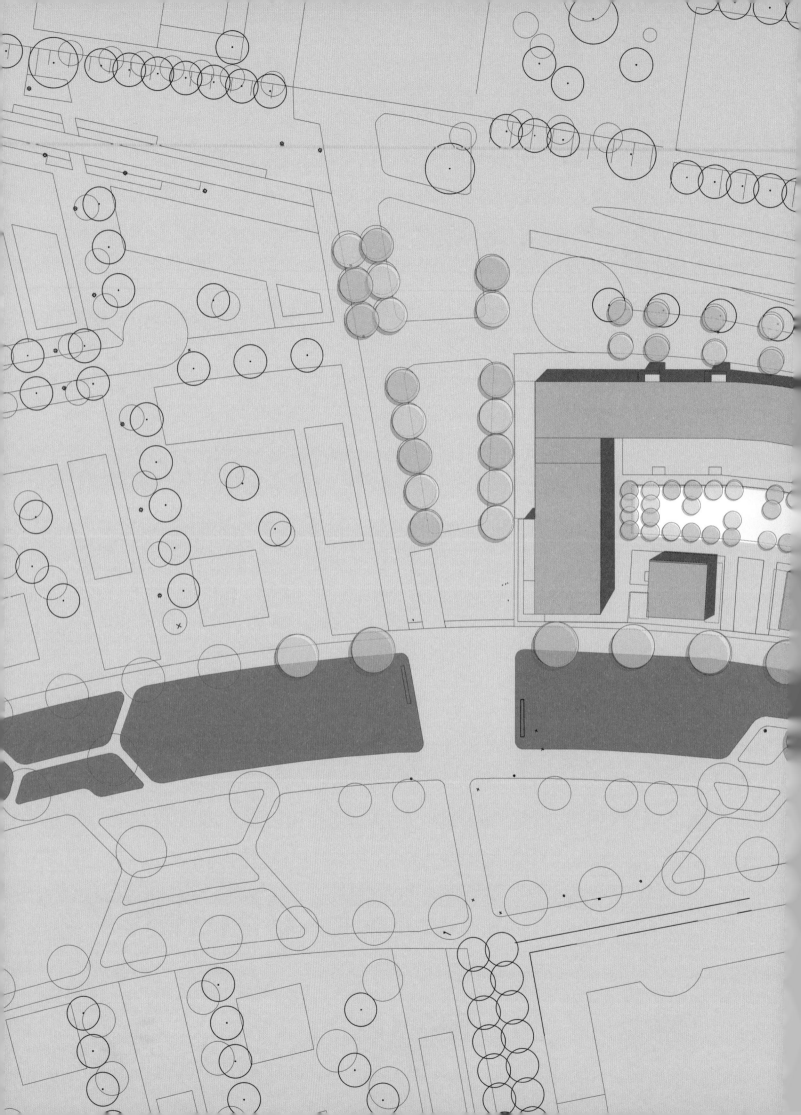

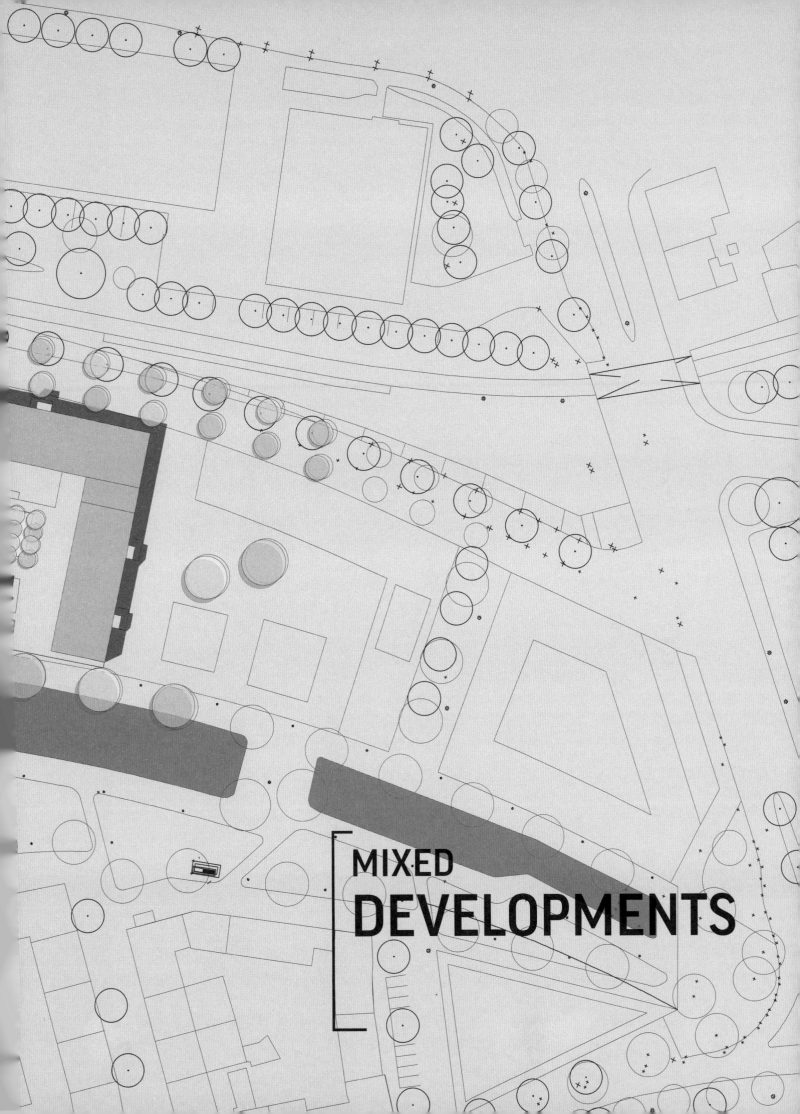

MIXED
DEVELOPMENTS

ICEBERG HOUSING
JDS / JULIEN DE SMEDT ARCHITECTS | CEBRA | SEARCH | LOUIS PAILLARD

LOCATION: MARIANE THOMSENS GADE, AARHUS, DENMARK | **COMPLETION:** 2013 | **CLIENT:** PENSIONDANMARK | **PHOTOGRAPHER:** JULIEN LANOO

For the Iceberg housing the design team reshaped the master plan that consisted of closed blocks, into four L-shaped wings. Its peaks and canyons render the project somehow playful, while granting all apartments a generous amount of natural light and views of the waterfront. At seven and eight stories and 21,500 square meters, the Iceberg houses one or two-floor apartments with commercial space on the ground floor. A variety of different apartment types results from the specific building shapes. Several two-story townhouses are integrated into the volume at ground level, while penthouse apartments are located on top of the buildings. The balconies feature glass with hues ranging from deep blue at the base to transparent at the top, resembling the color of an iceberg. A mix of apartments with different balconies, shapes and orientations ensures a socially diverse urban living environment.

OUTSTANDING DESIGN
ABOVE ALL, ISBJERGET, THE ORIGINAL NAME OF THE ICEBERG, HAS AN EYE-CATCHING APPEARANCE. ITS WHITE FAÇADES WITH ICE BLUE GLAZED BALCONIES AND SHARP PEAKS CONSTITUTE A LANDMARK AT THE OUTERMOST HARBOR FRONT OF AARHUS.

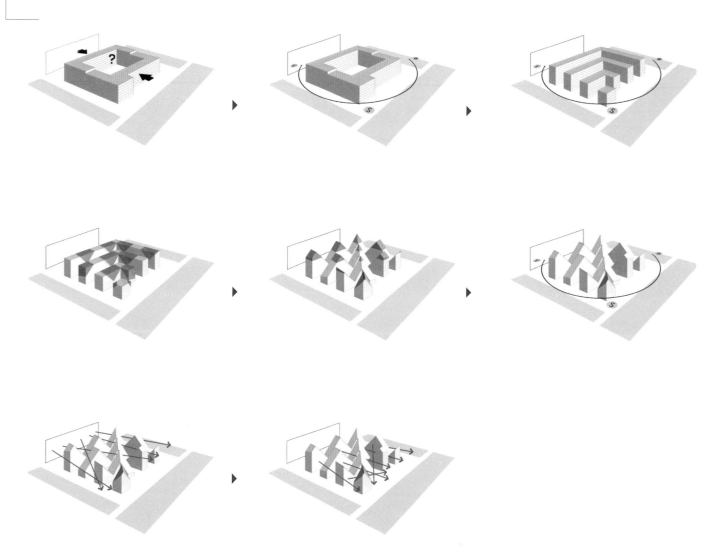

FACTS
SITE SIZE: 6,200 SQM
GFA TOTAL: 21,600 SQM
NO. BUILDINGS: 4
NO. UNITS: 220
KIND OF UNITS: APARTMENTS, 2-STORY TOWNHOUSES AND PENTHOUSES
193 UNDERGROUND PARKING LOTS
COMMERCIAL SPACE ON THE GROUND FLOOR

The Iceberg is situated at the front of the Aarhus Harbor development, De Bynære Havnearealer. It was built on the plot of a former container terminal. JDS, SeARCH, Louis Paillard and CEBRA created this spectacular project after winning a limited design competition in 2008. The entire area including the Iceberg is planned as a living city quarter, offering a multitude of cultural and social activities, 12,000 work places, and a highly mixed and diverse array of housing types which will accommodate 7,000 inhabitants. The Iceberg was one of the first completed projects. As a third of its apartments are reserved for affordable rental housing, it already contributes to social diversity in the new neighborhood.

COLLECTIVE ECO-HOUSING
LA CANOPÉE
PATRICK AROTCHAREN
AGENCE D'ARCHITECTURE

LOCATION: ZAC DU SÉQUÉ, 64100 BAYONNE, FRANCE | **COMPLETION:** 2011 | **CLIENT:** LE COL | **PHOTOGRAPHER:** VINCENT MONTHIERS AND MATHIEU CHOISELAT

This site, bounded by a protected natural wood-land, achieves an overall site density of 79 housing elements per hectare. An advanced 3D site study was carried out to find the exact placement for the housing units so that each living space could profit from year-round sunshine and views of the surrounding countryside. The 50 housing units are interconnected by raised timber walkways. The timber walkways erected at first floor level, flirting with the tall trees, offer a sensory and dreamlike pathway amongst the vegetation. The landings are semi-private spaces only serving two housing units maximum and open to the natural backdrop. The general idea is to treat all the units as if they were individual dwellings, thus reducing the overall visual density. All the buildings have a double orientation with an entirely glazed living space (six meters long) orientated mainly south, extendable by a private timber external balcony space (12 square meters). The kitchen and service areas open out onto this open area. The sleeping spaces are grouped on the higher levels, separated acoustically from the living spaces, both internally and externally by compact storage areas. Apart from the single-level two-bedroom apartments, the bathrooms and toilets are located on the north façades and are all naturally lit and ventilated.

FACTS
SITE SIZE: 6,350 SQM
GFA TOTAL: 3,800 SQM
NO. BUILDINGS: 50
NO. UNITS: 50
KIND OF UNITS: 12 INDIVIDUAL FAMILY HOMES,
3 GROUPS OF 3-4 APARTMENTS, 2 GROUPS OF
12 AND 16 APARTMENTS ON THE THIRD LEVEL
60 INDIVIDUAL PARKING LOTS

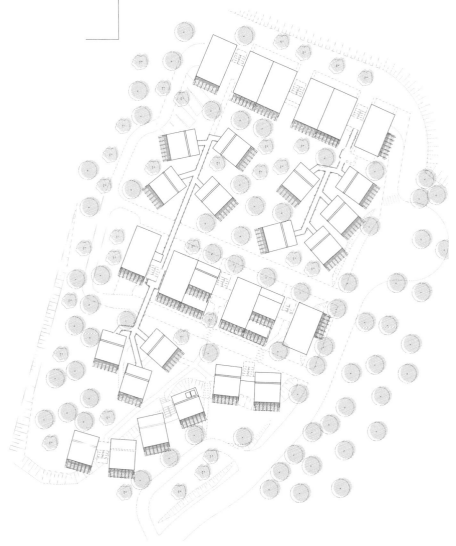

The urban development area of Sequé consists of a semi-urban eco zone situated in the hills just above the city of Bayonne in south-western France. The site and its landscape are idyllic; sitting in a clearing between rolling hills, on the edge of a forest surrounded by tall poplar trees planted for the previously existing municipal campsite. It is a leafy green haven, moments away from the city center. This collective housing project draws its inspiration from the traditional Basque wood

pigeon hunting huts built up in the trees, a game of architecture and nature, to create a poetic habitat and ever-changing environment with spectacular views and pathways. La Canopée complies with all the latest energy requirements. Locally sourced materials were used for the construction (pine from the surrounding forests and cellular concrete, also a locally produced material).

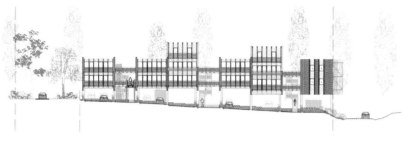

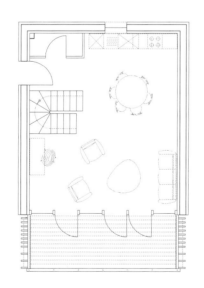
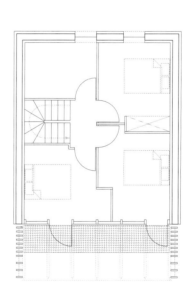

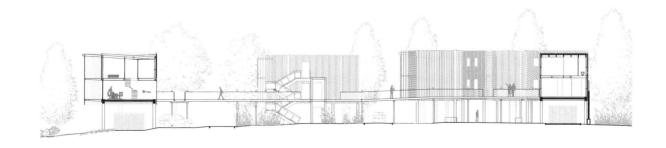

ENVIRONMENTAL IMPACT
BUILT OF LOCALLY PRODUCED
MATERIALS AND INCORPORATED
IN THE SURROUNDING NATURE,
THIS COLLECTIVE ECO-HOUSING
PROJECT WAS DESIGNED TO CON-
TROL AND MANAGE ALL ENVIRON-
MENTAL IMPACTS.

BROADWAY HOUSING
KEVIN DALY ARCHITECTS

LOCATION: 2602 BROADWAY AVENUE, SANTA MONICA, CA 90404, USA | **COMPLETION:** 2012 | **CLIENT:** COMMUNITY CORPORATION OF SANTA MONICA | **LANDSCAPE DESIGN:** DRY DESIGN | **PHOTOGRAPHER:** IWAN BAAN

The design of Broadway Housing aggregates two- and three-bedroom units into four repeatable blocks, arranged in a pinwheel configuration around the site. Larger three-bedroom units are placed at ground level. Two-bedroom units are placed on the upper levels and are connected by latticed bridges that envelope a central, shared courtyard. After-school programs are offered in a cluster of community buildings with planted roofs. The three story residential buildings are scattered around the starfish-shaped internal courtyard with a planter that extends through the underground parking level, allowing mature Sycamore trees to thrive and shade the courtyard. The multilevel bridge connecting the four residential blocks resembles a lattice house and adds layers of privacy, yet providing views across the courtyard. The arrangement maximizes the opportunities of the layout, directing the views from sleeping spaces to the perimeter of the site. All of the units open to the central courtyard, providing natural ventilation for each unit. Besides the ventilation the entire site is engineered to collect all roof and surface rain water and pipe it to an underground 57,000-liter cistern where the water is clarified and used for landscape irrigation.

FACTS
SITE SIZE: 6,070 SQM
GFA TOTAL: 3,087 SQM
NO. BUILDINGS: 4
NO. UNITS: 33
KIND OF UNITS: 29× 2 BEDROOMS AND 14× 3 BEDROOMS
66 UNDERGROUND PARKING LOTS
2 COMMUNITY ROOMS

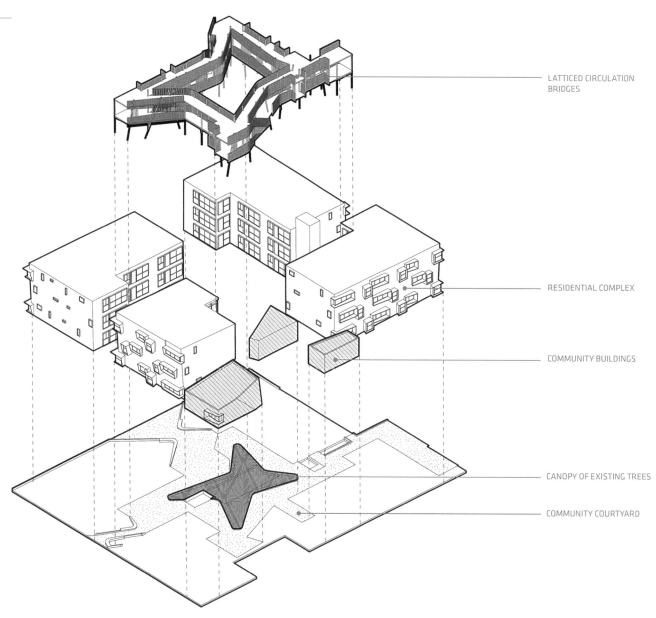

LATTICED CIRCULATION BRIDGES

RESIDENTIAL COMPLEX

COMMUNITY BUILDINGS

CANOPY OF EXISTING TREES

COMMUNITY COURTYARD

OPPORTUNITIES AND COMMUNITY
THE BROADWAY HOUSING'S FOUR BUILDINGS GATHER AROUND A CENTRAL COURTYARD. EACH UNIT OPENS TOWARDS THIS COMMUNITY SPACE. A COMMUNITY ZONE, COMPRISING TWO ROOMS, CAN BE USED FOR A VARIETY OF ACTIVITIES.

Developed by the Community Corporation of Santa Monica, Broadway Housing addresses the housing needs of families earning 30–60 percent of the local median income. The developer is committed to building and operating infill housing in Santa Monica, that is environmentally and economically sustainable. The city is known for progressive politics and daunting development regulations. The project, built on a 6,070-square-meter plot, replaces a vacant nursing home, adding density and activity to an urban corner site across from a large community park. The complex has access to a diverse range of transportation options including the future Bergamont Station Expo line and newly established bike lanes.

BILKER HÖFE
PINKARCHITEKTUR

LOCATION: FÄRBERSTRASSE, BRACHTSTRASSE, ESMARCHSTRASSE, 40223 DUSSELDORF, GERMANY | **COMPLETION:** 2013 | **CLIENT:** WOHNIMMOBILIE FÄRBERSTRASSE GMBH & CO. KG | **OPEN SPACE PLANNING:** PLANERGRUPPE OBERHAUSEN | **PHOTOGRAPHER:** MAX HAMPEL

The residential quarter Bilker Höfe turned a historical block with a historical career into the center of the lives of many young families. The listed former military hospital – possibly originally designed by Martin Gropius – remains the central orientation point and core of the design. Keeping a respectful distance, a car-free green island was created surrounding the classically designed courtyard area offering living space for all generations with 219 handicap-accessible residential units. The new buildings were designed to match the unique, multi-colored structured brick façade of the military hospital, which was listed in 1990. The plinths of the building are covered in clinker while the classical white plastered façades are structured horizontally by strips of light-gray molding. The façade structure is accentuated by anthracite-colored safety barriers shaped as abstract natural elements with frame and window elements in the same color. There is a great variety of apartment styles available – as the urban development structure can accommodate anything from one and two-room apartments, via residences for families, up to especially generously sized residential units – variety in unity.

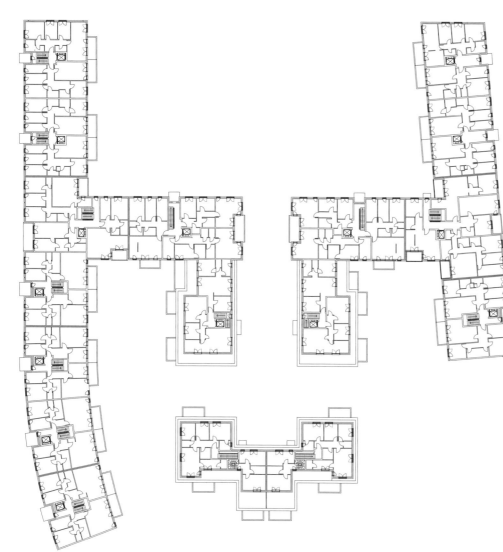

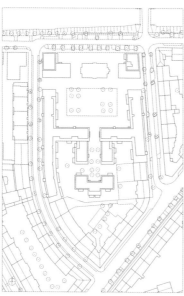

FACTS

SITE SIZE: 14,515 SQM

GFA TOTAL: 20,913 SQM

NO. BUILDINGS: 8

NO. UNITS: 219

ROAD LENGTH: 360 M

KIND OF UNITS: 2-5 ROOM APART-
MENTS, MAISONETTES, PENTHOUSES

NEIGHBORHOOD UNDERGROUND
PARKING FOR 279 CARS AND 300
BIKES

LISTED FORMER MILITARY HOSPITAL

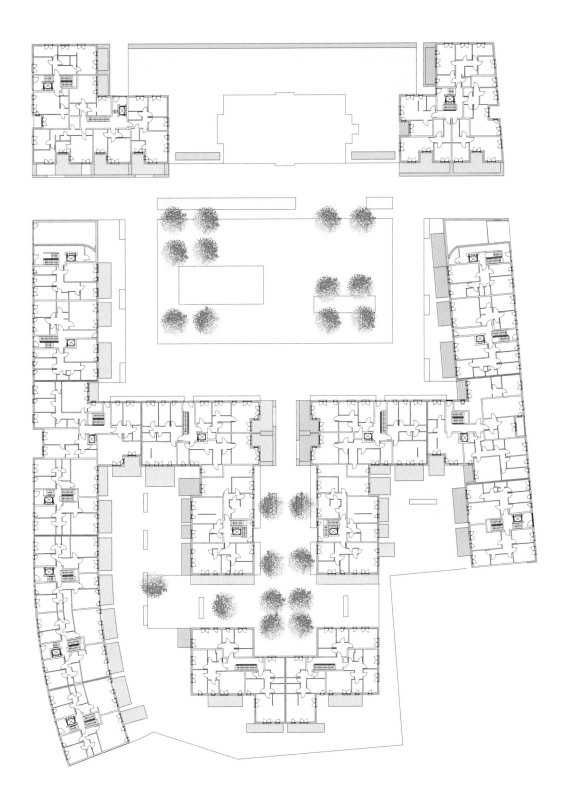

Despite its central location, excellent connection to public transportation net, local suppliers and cultural and education institutions, the premises on which the Bilker Höfe project is located were unused for a long period of time. Its development adds a new nucleus to the city quarter. Inspired by the layout of the former military hospital complex, the new buildings give shape to generously greened squares whose degree of private versus public use varies from north to south. The building heights are based on the standard height of the buildings along the streets and the buildings neighboring the listed old building match its height. On both sides of the largest district square the edges of the blocks are intercepted by pedestrian paths. This square is the green heart of the quarter, offering a haven of relaxation with children's playgrounds and recreational areas. Bilker Höfe received the DGNB (German Sustainable Building Council) certificate in gold.

QUARTER REVITALIZATION

REVITALIZATION TURNED THE QUARTER INTO A GREEN RESIDENTIAL ESTATE FOR ALL GENERATIONS. THE REAWAKENING OF UNDERUSED CITY QUARTERS TO FILL THEM WITH NEW AND SUSTAINED LIFE IS AMONG THE MOST THRILLING AND DEMANDING TASKS OF ARCHITECTURE AND URBAN PLANNING.

URBAN HYBRID
MVRDV

LOCATION: QUARTIER FELDBREITE, EMMEN, SWITZERLAND | **COMPLETION:** ONGOING |
CLIENT: SENN BPM AG, ST. GALLEN | **CO-ARCHITECTS:** GKS ARCHITEKTEN+PARTNER AG |
LANDSCAPE ARCHITECTS: FONTANA LANDSCHAFTSARCHITEKTUR | **VISUALIZATION:**
MVRDV

The exterior of the block is a varied urban street front whilst the interior offers the quality of a green and intimate village. The interior is divided into both private and public spaces, with dividing walls used for tables or benches. A cohesive landscaping plan foresees a wide variety of fruit trees in the courtyard, in both the private and public areas. The landscaping will attempt to blur the lines between the interior and exterior of the block into an extensive park-like format. The garden and patio houses in the center of the courtyard have their own entrance doors at the outer perimeter of the block. Parking for the block is underground to create a car-free interior and the roofs of the buildings will be used for additional outdoor space. An important aspect of the project is the high-quality construction combined with relatively low prices. Clients will be able to buy a more or less finished house with options leading up to almost full fit and finish. Homeowners with little money can therefore delay investment, or do the work themselves, and still live in a high-quality, newly built home. Each house or apartment will have its own façade color, emphasizing its individual ownership and individual floor plans. A pastel range of color was chosen based on the specific colors traditionally found in historic Swiss town centers in the Lucerne area.

FACTS
SITE SIZE: 4,968 SQM
GFA TOTAL: 9,000 SQM
NO. BUILDINGS: 37
NO. UNITS: 97
KIND OF UNITS: 16 TYPES OF HOUSING
UNITS IN 34 SINGLE-FAMILY HOUSES AND
3 APARTMENT BUILDINGS
UNDERGROUND PARKING

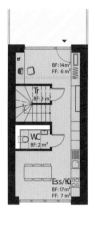
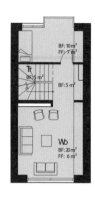

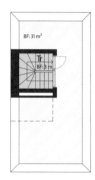

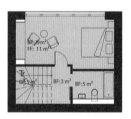
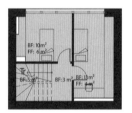

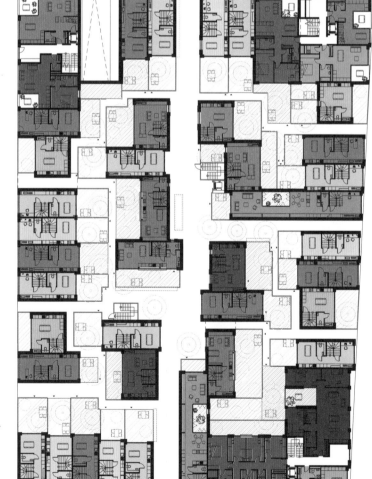

URBAN VILLAGE
THE URBAN BUILDING BLOCK IS TREATED
LIKE AN INDEPENDENT VILLAGE. A DENSE
NEIGHBORHOOD WILL ESTABLISH THE SOCIAL
LIFE AND ACTIVITIES OF A SMALL, CLOSED
COMMUNITY.

For the urban development area Feldbreite, located in Emmen, Switzerland, MVRDV created a permeable courtyard block with small apartment buildings at the corners, townhouses along the streets, and garden and patio houses inside the block instead of the monolithic housing block described by the brief. The 16 different housing types, which vary in size from 30 to 130 square meters and from one to four floors, provide an incredibly diverse variety of accommodations for different types of inhabitants. The houses are colored individually in a pastel pallet, which references historic buildings in the area.

LIVING AT PIER 78
KOSCHANY + ZIMMER ARCHITEKTEN KZA

LOCATION: MEYER-SCHWICKERATH-STRASSE 41–69, 45127 ESSEN, GERMANY |
COMPLETION: 2013 | **CLIENT:** ALLBAU AG | **LANDSCAPE DESIGN:** PLAN B
JÜRGENSMANN LANDERS | **PHOTOGRAPHER:** DANIEL SUMESGUTNER

The different building types of PIER 78, a U-shaped structure with two added detached houses and underground parking, surround a clearly structured, landscaped inner courtyard with seating, children's playground, and tenant gardens. Parts of the building are located directly at the waterfront and the park promenade. Plastered façades with playfully arranged balconies define the view from the north and the east. Towards the south and the west, the residents can enjoy floor-to-ceiling height patio windows with individually adjustable sun screens that offer a marvelous view of the promenade. The building was constructed from masonry and concrete – the basement floor and the underground parking as a watertight concrete structure and the four top floors of brickwork with reinforced concrete pillars and ceilings. KZA constructed the residential complex according to the German energy efficiency standard KfW 70. Heating is provided as district heating. The buildings are designed with large glazing sections towards the south and the west, as well as perforated façades to the north and east, also contributing positively to the energy efficiency. All buildings have green roofs. PIER 78 has been awarded the German Property Developer Prize 2014 and the Award for Architecture of the City of Essen 2015.

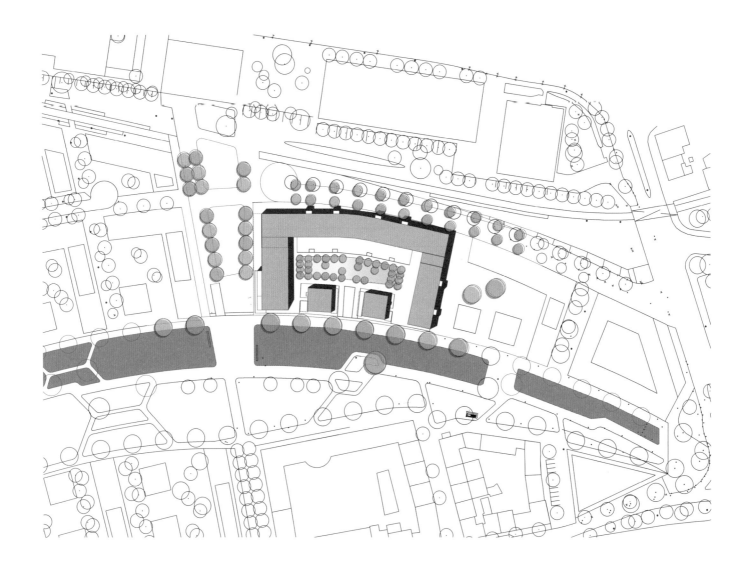

PIER 78 is part of a more than four-hectare-large revitalized commercial wasteland, the new "green center of Essen", situated between downtown Essen and the University of Duisburg-Essen. This newly developed, urban high-quality quarter with a central park, extensive green and water areas, promenades and public squares ensures a high-quality urban landscape. The residential buildings can be distinguished by their orientation to the public parks and squares with commercial areas, cafés, and outdoor restaurants. This particularly highlights their prominent location on the main connection and central axis between the university and downtown, while supporting the central square as the center of the entire complex.

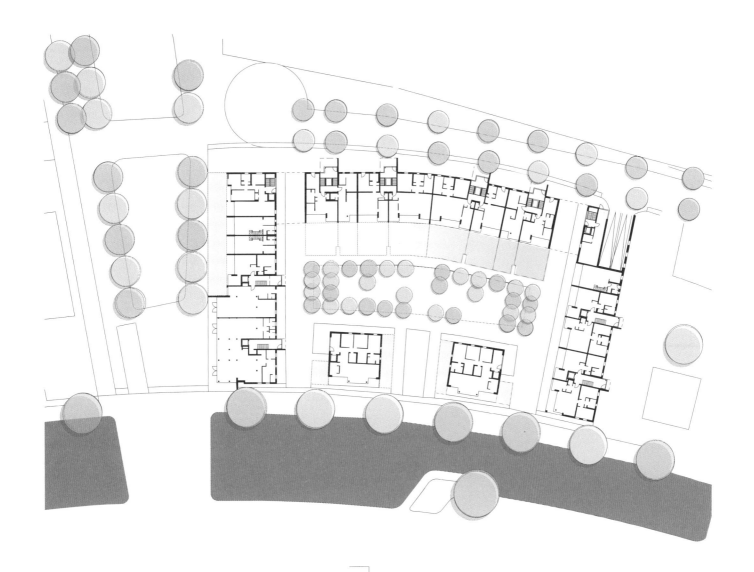

FACTS

SITE SIZE: 7,805 SQM
GFA TOTAL: 7,500 SQM
NO. BUILDINGS: 3
NO. UNITS: 77
ROAD LENGTH: 280 M
INHABITANTS: 160
KIND OF UNITS: 1–3 BEDROOMS
92 UNDERGROUND PARKING LOTS
COMMERCIAL AND RECREATIONAL SPACES

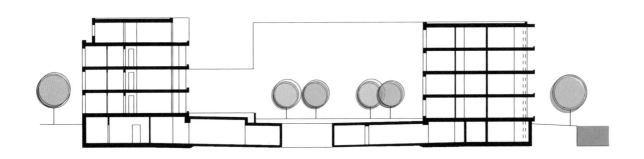

LIVING NEAR THE WATER
THE RESIDENTIAL AREA AT PIER 78
WAS BUILT ON FORMER INNER-CITY
COMMERCIAL WASTELAND. THE
STAGGERED BUILDING ARRANGE-
MENTS ALLOW VIEWS OF THE RIVER
AND THE PARK PROMENADE FROM
ALMOST ALL APARTMENTS.

SUSTAINABLE SOCIAL HOUSING DISTRICT SINT-AGATHA-BERCHEM
BURO II & ARCHI+I

LOCATION: 10/44, RUE DE LA GÉRANCE AND 37/49, RUE TERMONDE, 1083 BERCHEM-SAINTE-AGATHE, BELGIUM | **COMPLETION:** 2012 | **CLIENT:** SOCIÉTÉ DU LOGEMENT DE LA RÉGION BRUXELLES-CAPITAL (SLRB) | **PHOTOGRAPHER:** FILIP DUJARDIN

The volumes and maximum building heights echo the buildings created by Victor Bourgeois in his Cité Moderne and its style of canopies, balconies, patios, and awnings. The contemporary translation of these modernistic elements ensures a sufficient variety in typology for the eight different blocks. As a mark of honor for the revolutionary use of concrete by Victor Bourgeois, the façades have been provided with an outer covering of precast concrete. In combination with wood this creates a warm contrast. The choice of flat roofs completes the cubist context of the Cité Moderne.

This sustainable district guarantees a balance between economic, technical, and social criteria and offers both high architectural quality and excellent energy performance rates using solar panels, rainwater recovery, environmentally friendly materials as well as optimized insulation and ventilation. The apartments and the houses have a K-value of 30.

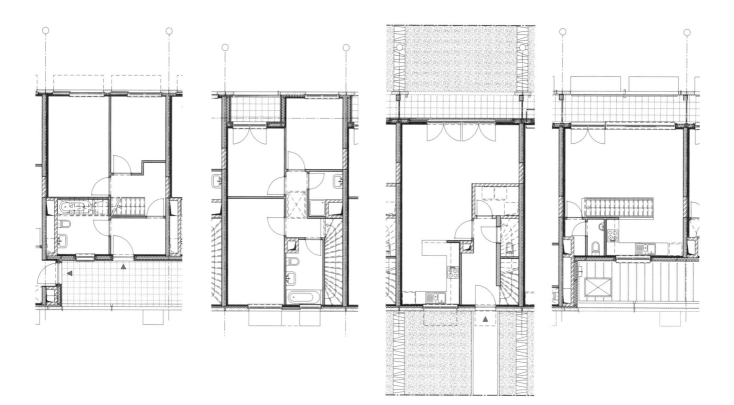

FACTS
SITE SIZE: 13,670 SQM
GFA TOTAL: 8,328 SQM
NO. BUILDINGS: 32
NO. UNITS: 75
ROAD LENGTH: 266 M
INHABITANTS: 300
KIND OF UNITS: 1–5 BEDROOMS
49 OUTDOOR PARKING LOTS

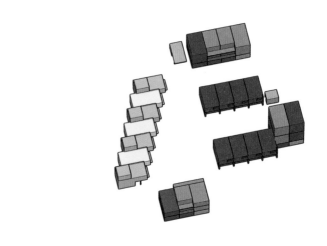

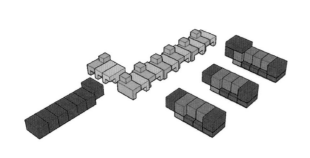

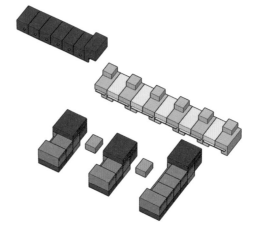

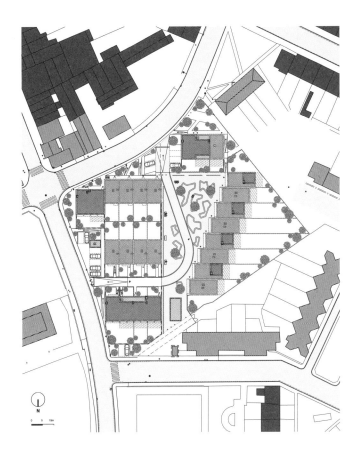

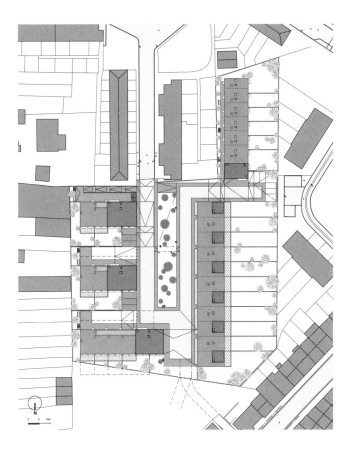

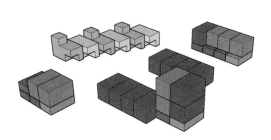

Sint-Agatha-Berchem/Berchem-Sainte-Agathe is a north-western district of Bruxelles. These new social housing units were designed in addition to the cubist social housing district Cité Moderne, built in 1922–1925 by architect Victor Bourgeois. One plot is located along the Beheersstraat and has 43 units, the other one is along the Dendermondestraat with 32 units. On both plots, four blocks of apartments and low-energy houses have been built, classically aligned or in a saw tooth config-uration. Low walls and hedges define the imme-diate environment and the property boundaries between the residences and the common area. The layout of the common area is to a high standard, in line with what L. Van der Swaelm has achieved in the Cité Moderne. The courtyard, with its benches and greenery, invites residents and visitors to meet and interact.

AN ECOLOGICAL CITÉ MODERNE
THE PROJECT CONSISTS OF SUSTAINABLE AND CONTEMPORARY TRANSLATIONS OF THE MODERNIST ELEMENTS OF VICTOR BOURGEOIS.

ESTATE BUCHHEIMER WEG
ASTOC ARCHITECTS AND PLANNERS

LOCATION: BUCHHEIMER WEG, 51107 COLOGNE, GERMANY | **COMPLETION:** 2012 |
CLIENT: GAG IMMOBILIEN AG, COLOGNE | **PHOTOGRAPHER:** CHRISTA LACHENMAIER
(197 A.), JENS WILLEBRAND

ASTOC provided the rows of the existing settlement with a bend in the center, so that two rows each point towards and away from each other. This seemingly simple intervention resulted in major improvements – the spaces between the rows are loosely framed without creating the problems of perimeter block development, as the two plans on page ten show. This resulted in alternating greened inner courtyards and genuine semi-public courtyards. The pitched roofs were replaced by a tilted roof style and the traditionally central roof ridge was diagonally moved to the outer corners of the building, resulting in the characteristic rising and falling eaves. To express the new mentality with a fresher design, all houses are clad in mineral plastered façades in five different shades of light green. Across the complex the hue changes from very light to darker green, with two shades on every house and a change in color on the building corners and bend lines. The affordable rent including heat remained the same despite significantly larger layouts and the addition of two new elevators. As standard, two apartments are accessed by a staircase, while on the edges of the buildings three apartments share a staircase. The residential quarter was enhanced by vitalizing infrastructure facilities such as a renters' café, nearby offices and a three-group child daycare facility plus a home for people with disabilities and a residential group of people suffering from dementia.

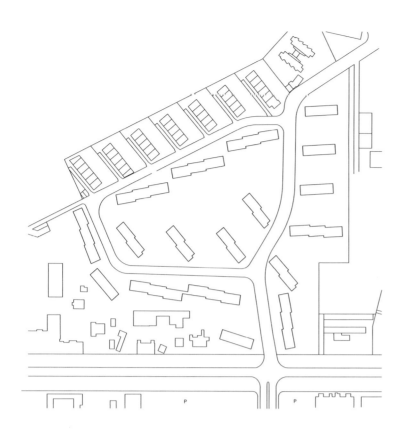

FACTS
SITE SIZE: 42,000 SQM
GFA TOTAL: 51,600 SQM
NO. BUILDINGS: 18
NO. UNITS: 434
ROAD LENGTH: 652 M
INHABITANTS: 1,100
KIND OF UNITS: 1–3 BEDROOMS
350 LOTS IN PARKING SPACES AND
PARKING GARAGE
CAFÉ, DAYCARE CENTER, HOME FOR
HANDICAPPED PEOPLE

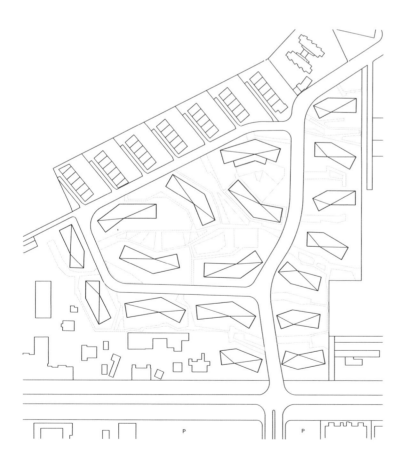

The row construction style of German residential complexes of the 1950s offered little less than affordable living space and extensive unstructured greened areas. In terms of urban development, their weaknesses consisted of unidentifiable street and outdoor areas, and hard to find addresses. Nowadays, the inherited complexes of the 1950s and 1960s are suddenly receiving much attention – many of these complexes must be technically renovated and too small layouts need to be revised.

The aim is to maintain the affordable housing for low income families while improving the indoor and outdoor urban development qualities. AS-TOC's design for the reconstruction of the complex near Buchheimer Weg maintained the advantages of row construction – good illumination, ventilation and orientation while adding better spatial characteristics and gradated outdoor areas. It can serve as a model for other complexes of the kind, in Cologne and elsewhere.

IMPROVING EXISTING SPACE

THE DESIGN FOR THE ESTATE NEAR BUCHHEIMER WEG IN COLOGNE IS A CRITICAL CONTINUATION OF THE RESIDENTIAL COMPLEX CONCEPTS OF THE 1950S AND A MODEL FOR IMPROVING THE QUALITY OF RESIDENTIAL AND LIVING SPACES OF A HOUSING ESTATE IN A SOCIALLY CHALLENGED CITY DISTRICT.

MARBLE ARCH
MORPHOGENESIS

LOCATION: MANIMAJRA, CHANDIGARH-160101, INDIA | **COMPLETION:** 2010 | **CLIENT:** UPPAL GROUP HOUSING | **PHOTOGRAPHER:** JATINDER MARWAHA (202 A.), ANDRE J FANTHOME

The guiding principle for the project was the commitment to rely as much as possible on natural resources such as daylight, natural ventilation, passive cooling, and water recycling. The built volumes of the residential strips were sculpted to provide terraces and open areas at all levels to generate interaction between each building and its direct surroundings. The built form was generated by creating a pedestrian area for the apartments at the center of the site. This was achieved by moving all traffic to the periphery. The pedestrian area was laid out with strips of defined functions

for residential facilities, services, and recreation areas extending from east to west, which allowed all apartments to be optimally aligned in a north-south orientation to accommodate natural daylight and ventilation. The development has been configured as a set of nine blocks of five stories each with four apartments to a level and service courtyards straddled as buffers for a total of 168 units. The development also includes ancillary facilities such as a health club, gymnasium, amphitheater, swimming pool, and social activity areas.

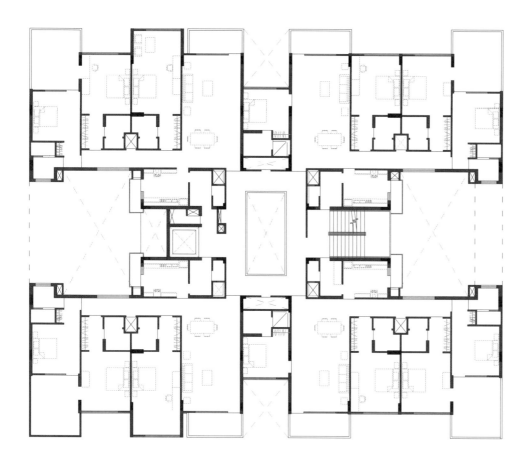

FACTS
SITE SIZE: 21,853 SQM
GFA TOTAL: 39,950 SQM
NO. BUILDINGS: 3
NO. UNITS: 168
ROAD LENGTH: 580 M
INHABITANTS: 600
KIND OF UNITS: 3-4-BEDROOM APARTMENTS, PENTHOUSES
336 BASEMENT PARKING LOTS

For a densely populated country like India, the conventional idea of a plot of land with a detached single-family dwelling will eventually become a rarity. This project's aim was to develop a new prototype for housing in Chandigarh, shifting away from the archetypal morphology of high-specification residential modules and equipment crammed into undersized apartments. The 'bungalow' is being increasingly replaced by mixed use developments. The most common typical dwelling unit in most large cities across the world is now an apartment. To protect the ecosystem, the future may require high-rises with independent, self-sufficient, stacked micro communities that form a part of an overall city. Marble Arch, built on a 22,000-square-meter site, explores the boundaries of retaining the urban character of Chandigarh, the capital of Punjab and Haryana, while leaving a distinguished mark on the city.

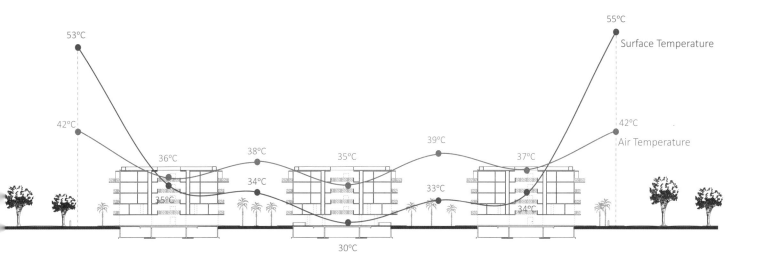

53°C
42°C
36°C
35°C
34°C
38°C
35°C
34°C
39°C
33°C
37°C
34°C
30°C
55°C
Surface Temperature
42°C
Air Temperature

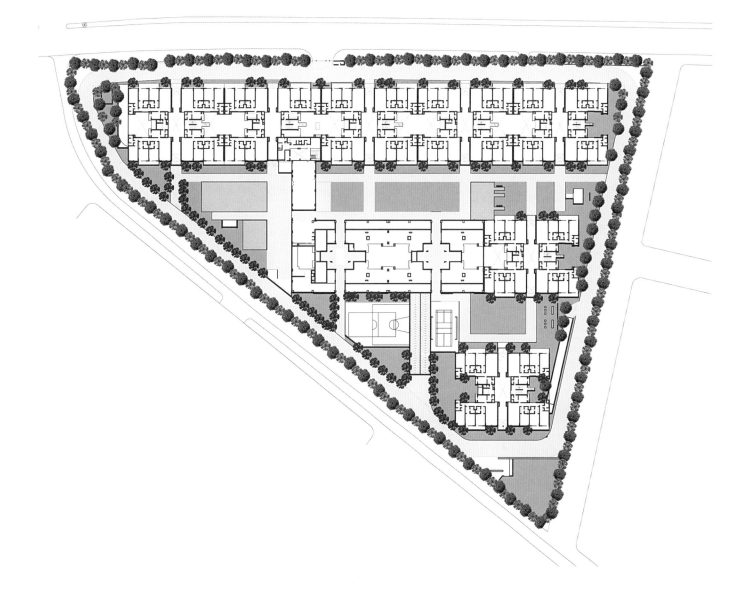

NEW PROTOTYPE

THE PROJECT'S OBJECTIVE IS TO DEVELOP A NEW PROTOTYPE FOR HOUSING AS AN ENTITY IN CHANDIGARH TO ADDRESS ISSUES OF LIVABILITY, SPATIAL CONFIGURATION, ENVIRONMENTAL AND SOCIAL ISSUES, WHILE SHIFTING TO MID-RISE MID-DENSITY, AS AGAINST THE ARCHETYPAL HIGH-RISE MORPHOLOGY.

SOPHIENTERRASSEN
PINKARCHITEKTUR
LOCATION: HARVESTEHUDER STIEG 5-11 AND 21-24, PARKVILLA 2, 20149 HAMBURG,
GERMANY | **COMPLETION:** 2014 | **CLIENT:** FRANKONIA EUROBAU AG |
OPEN SPACE PLANNING: WES & PARTNER LANDSCHAFTSARCHITEKTEN |
PHOTOGRAPHER: MARTIN KUNZE

On the Sophienhöhe, the former German armed forces premises near the Außenalster in Hamburg, the Sophienterrassen consist of 137 residential units and 6,000 square meters of office space. pinkarchitektur has contributed townhouses and urban villas to the project. In reference to Classical Modernity, the shape and material language of the architecture is understated and clearly structured. It mostly employs glass, whitewashed façades, aluminum and precious wood. The choice of these light-colored materials give the houses an elegant shine amid the protected old trees.

The townhouses in the center of the compound consist of a row of urban houses that are either used by single owners across three levels plus a penthouse, or consist of two "stacked houses" that are designed in the duplex style, connecting either the ground and second floor or the third and fourth floor.

Each townhouse has its own backyard. The residence styles and sizes of the urban villas can be combined in a modular way and the ceiling heights of the individual buildings and apartments were deliberately chosen 3.50 meters high. The omnipresence of greenery can be found above the ground as well: all new buildings have flat roofs with timber floor boards or green roofs.

FACTS

SITE SIZE: 9,100 SQM
GFA TOTAL: 6,567 SQM
NO. BUILDINGS: 3
NO. UNITS: 25
KIND OF UNITS: 2-4-BEDROOM APARTMENTS,
SINGLE-FAMILY HOUSES, MAISONETTES
39 UNDERGROUND PARKING LOTS

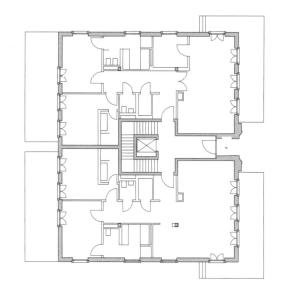

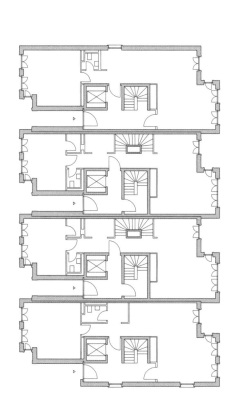

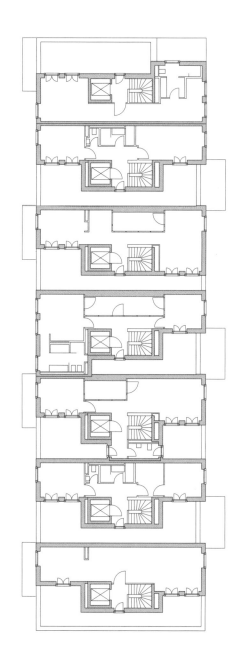

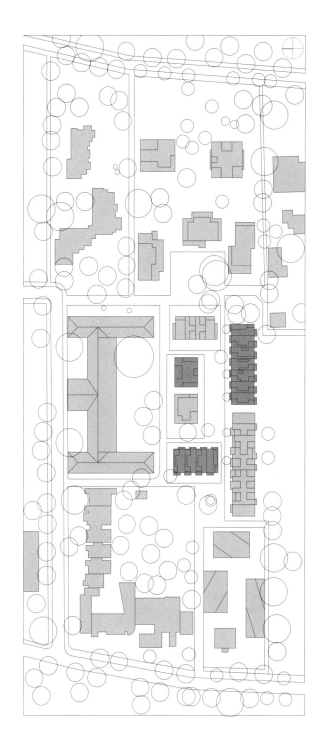

The Sophienterrassen residential project is located north of downtown Hamburg, on the western bank of the Außenalster. Away from the public eye since the 1930s, it was used by the National Socialist regime as a gendarmerie general command and later by the German armed forces as an administrative domicile. It only became publicly accessible again in the course of German reunification. The Sophienterrassen project is dominated by the characteristic features of the Alster region – a sequence of paths and squares all the way to the river, old, protected trees and the houses of the Außenalster quarters that have traditionally been whitewashed since the 19th century. The basic urban development concept of the Sophienterrassen is a sequence of connected squares that are framed by the quarter's houses.

PURE AND ELEGANT
THE ARCHITECTURAL SHAPES
AND THE USED MATERIALS
ARE REDUCED AND PURE
– BASED ON CLASSICAL MOD-
ERNISM AND INSPIRED BY THE
SELF-CONFIDENT HAMBURG
BOURGEOISIE. THE TYPES AND
SIZES OF THE TOWNHOUSES
AND URBAN VILLAS CAN BE
COMBINED IN A MODULAR WAY.

FROHHEIM RESIDENTIAL ESTATE
MÜLLER SIGRIST ARCHITEKTEN | EM2N ARCHITEKTEN

LOCATION: IM BÖDEN 45-87, WEHNTALERSTRASSE 464-482, 8046 ZURICH, SWITZERLAND | **COMPLETION:** 2012 | **CLIENT:** BAUGENOSSENSCHAFT FROHHEIM | **LANDSCAPE ARCHITECT:** ANDREA FAHRLÄNDER DIA LANDSCHAFTSARCHITEKTUR | **COLOR CONCEPT:** JÖRG NIEDERBERGER | **PHOTOGRAPHER:** ROGER FREI, MÜLLER SIGRIST ARCHITEKTEN AG (215 A.)

With its continuous semi-basement and point structures, the longitudinal Frohheim complex creates an urban development counterpoint to the public greened space. The aim was not to construct a noise insulation wall but instead a constructed border to the street as a natural element of the entire superstructure. The ground floor of the two-story "noise insulation bar" is modeled on inner city areas with stores, service establishments and two child daycare facilities. The point buildings behind them contain three apartments per floor that are accessed by wide ramps and entrance halls as well as naturally illuminated staircases. The mix of 132 apartments includes duplexes with private atriums in the elongated building. The apartments in the point houses are aligned in various directions and feature large balconies. These extend drawer-like from the building and are horizontally offset to each other, creating two-story outdoor areas. Along with the colored railings and metallic window frames, these balconies structure the buildings. Inside the apartments, the layouts remain flexible due to the omission of non-bearing room separating walls and can be adjusted to future needs.

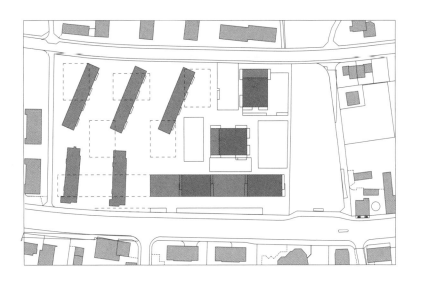

FACTS
SITE SIZE: 16,914 SQM
GFA TOTAL: 29,972 SQM
NO. BUILDINGS: 8
NO. UNITS: 132
ROAD LENGTH: 320 M
KIND OF UNITS: 1-4 BEDROOMS
161 UNDERGROUND PARKING LOTS
STORES, SERVICE ESTABLISHMENTS
AND TWO CHILD DAYCARE FACILITIES

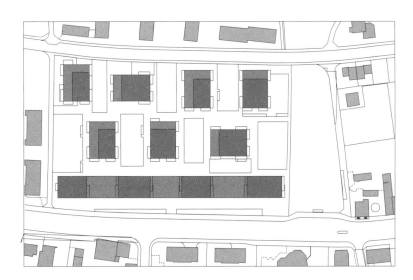

The Frohheim settlement is located in the Affoltern community in the Swiss canton of Zurich. The main characteristic of Affoltern is its greened loose settlement structure based on the green city concepts and plans of Albert Heinrich Steiner, the former town master mason. The high-traffic Wehntalerstrasse constitutes the backbone of this relatively homogeneous settlement structure, with the main central functions located next to and constructed along it. The renovation of the Frohheim complex provided the chance to create another sub-center along this street. The new superstructure matches the grain and formats of the existing settlement structures, customized to optimally fit into the context.

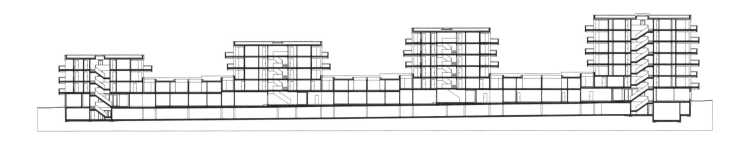

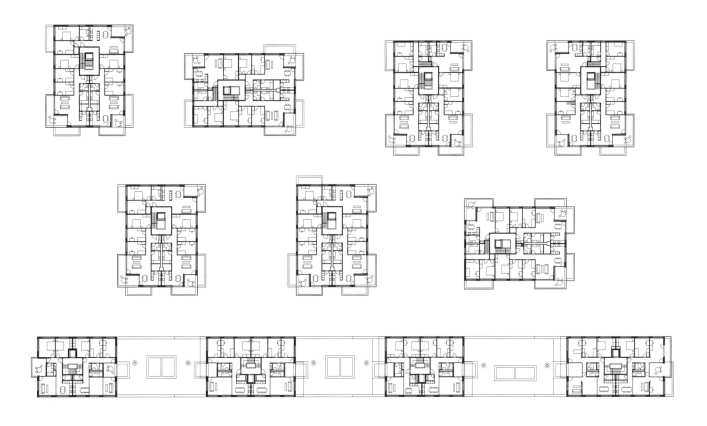

RHYTHM

EVENLY POSITIONED, BRIGHTLY COLORED EXTENDING BALCONIES ON VARIOUS FLOORS ARE THE SCULPTURED STRUCTURES OF THIS LITTLE CITY IN THE CITY THAT OFFERS ITS RESIDENTS HIGH RESIDENTIAL QUALITY COUPLED WITH COST EFFICIENCY.

WOODEN HOUSING BLOCK
BERGER + PARKKINEN ARCHITEKTEN | QUERKRAFT ARCHITEKTEN

LOCATION: MARIA-TUSCH-STRASSE 6, 1220 VIENNA, AUSTRIA | **COMPLETION:** 2015 | **CLIENT:** EBG GEMEINNÜTZIGE EIN- UND MEHRFAMILIENHÄUSER BAUGENOSSENSCHAFT REG. GEN.M.B.H. | **LANDSCAPE ARCHITECTS:** IDEALICE | **PHOTOGRAPHER:** HERTHA HURNAUS

The housing complex consists of seven building parts ranging in height from four to seven floors above ground level and an underground parking. The edges of the ground floor zone are formed by a two-story multi-functional ring, which incorporates commercial uses, communal spaces, and studio apartments. The inner courtyard is a semi-public zone that forms the common heart of the complex, which is connected to the pedestrian zone and is surrounded at ground floor level by the communal rooms. This so-called canyon, an area with several different levels and seating steps at the heart of the complex, offers residents an opportunity to meet and experience a feeling of community. Wing-shaped terraces form an organic landscape together with a number of grassy hillocks. Hills, trees, and shrubs with small crowns screen the private terraces. The external prefabricated timber walls are produced using native wood and wood-based materials. Thanks to the high level of prefabrication and speedy assembly on site, the impact on the environment can be minimized. The concrete frame allows freedom in designing the façade and permanent flexibility in the floor plans.

FACTS

SITE SIZE: 7,700 SQM
GFA TOTAL: 37,450 SQM
NO. BUILDINGS: 7
NO. UNITS: 213
ROAD LENGTH: 320 M
KIND OF UNITS: 1-4-BEDROOM APART-
MENTS, ATELIERS
412 BASEMENT PARKING LOTS
8 SHOPS, COMMUNAL SPACES

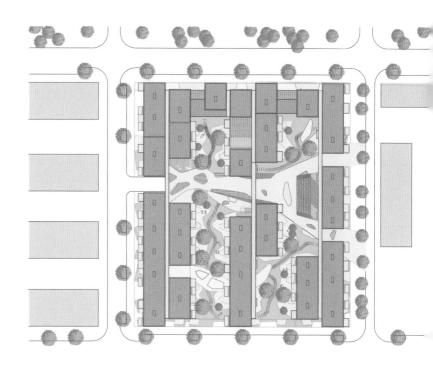

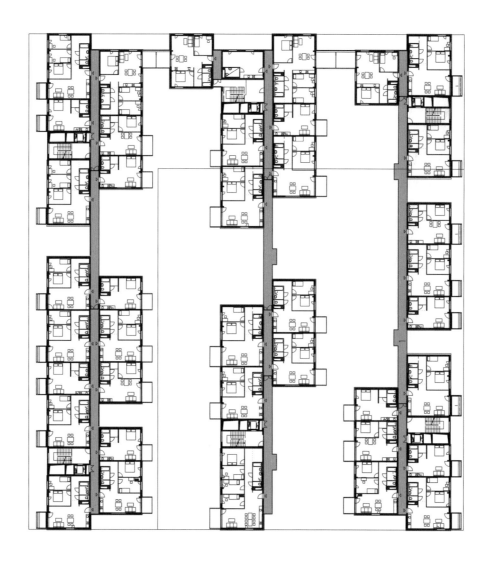

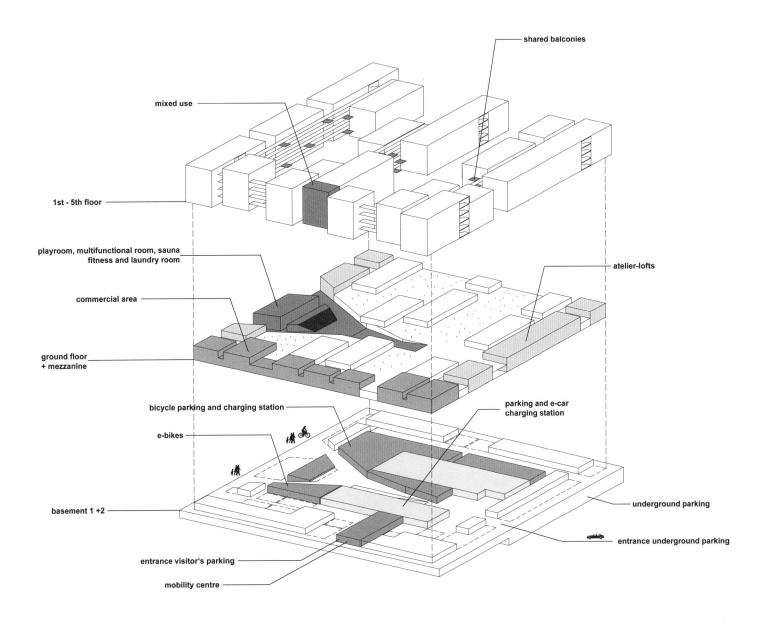

shared balconies

mixed use

1st - 5th floor

playroom, multifunctional room, sauna
fitness and laundry room

atelier-lofts

commercial area

ground floor
+ mezzanine

bicycle parking and charging station

parking and e-car
charging station

e-bikes

underground parking

basement 1 +2

entrance underground parking

entrance visitor's parking

mobility centre

The Seestadt Aspern is a large urban development area in the north-east of the Austrian capital of Vienna. Until 2028, a total of 10,500 apartments and 20,000 workstations will be built on 240 hectares. Fifty percent of the total area is reserved for green and leisure zones. In the south-eastern part of the Seestadt, the architects are using a large building plot for a sequence of parallel building volumes with various scales. The complex with 213 apartments and 8 shops consists of a group of clearly recognizable individual timber houses in the form of slender, compact individual volumes. The various parts are connected to each other by three rows of access decks that run in a north-south direction. These three circulation routes provide a sequence of light-flooded staircases, internal corridors and open access decks to which communal terraces are docked.

MULTIFUNCTIONALITY
A MULTIFUNCTIONAL TWO-FLOOR BASE LEVEL OF MIXED USE CONNECTS THE HOUSING ESTATE. ITS HEART IS THE SEMI-PUBLIC COURTYARD WITH WOODEN RAMPS AND TERRACED SEATING AREAS.

NINETREE VILLAGE
DAVID CHIPPERFIELD ARCHITECTS

LOCATION: WUYUN ZHONG ROAD, HANGZHOU, CHINA | **COMPLETION:** 2008 | **CLIENT:** ZHEJIANG JOYON REAL ESTATE CO. LTD. | **LANDSCAPE ARCHITECTS:** LEVIN MONSIGNY LANDSCHAFTSARCHITEKTEN, ZHEJIANG GREENTOWN LANDSCAPE CONSTRUCTION | **PHOTOGRAPHER:** CHRISTIAN RICHTERS, SHU HE (226 B.)

The development contains six types of buildings differing in size and floor plan, depending on the location, view, and light conditions. The individual apartment buildings contain five generously proportioned apartments, each accommodating a full floor of approximately 450 square meters. The floor plan concept creates a flowing interior space defined by solid elements that accommodate auxiliary functions. The selection of materials for the living and sleeping areas provides an elegant, calm atmosphere, whilst the enclosed elements are designed as cabinets using precious traditional materials. The loggia zone, which runs around the whole building, provides a transition area between the interior living space and the sur-

rounding nature. Based on a traditional principle of Chinese housing, an exterior skin using wooden elements protects the privacy of the residents. This skin differs in density, depending on the interior functions, sunlight, and the conditions of the site. Moveable elements allow the residents to further decide on the desired degree of privacy.

Skylights let natural light deep into the rooms. In front of the small clubhouse lies a raised platform with an irregular shape following the natural borders of the site. The building is made out of colored concrete and Chinese volcanic stone.

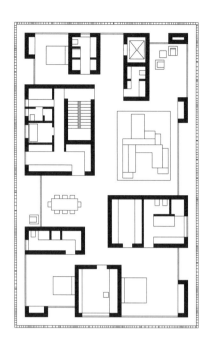

FACTS
SITE SIZE: 16,000 SQM
GFA TOTAL: 23,500 SQM
NO. BUILDINGS: 12
NO. UNITS: 60
KIND OF UNITS: 6 TYPES
UNDERGROUND PARKING
CLUBHOUSE

N

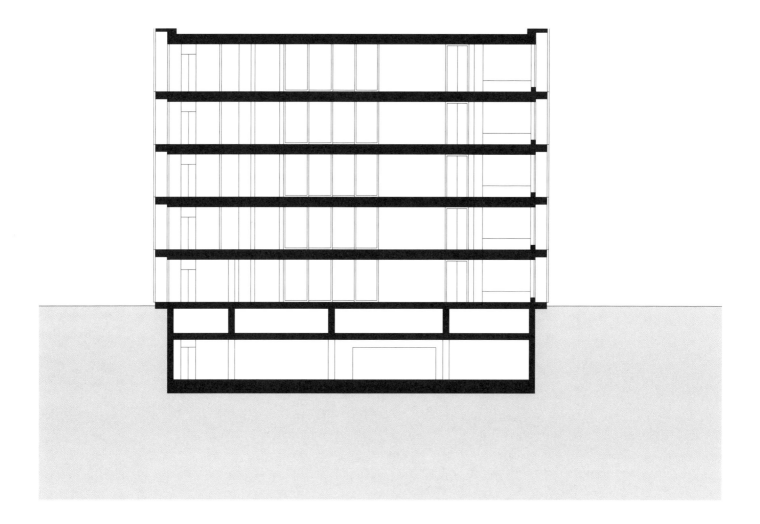

A small valley, bordered by a dense bamboo forest, forms the site for this luxury housing development, situated near the Qiang Tang River in Hangzhou, in south-eastern China. Twelve individual volumes are arranged in a chessboard pattern to create maximum open space for each building. Each apartment building has been set in its own clearing in the forest and adapts to the topography, creating a flowing landscape via a slight turn of the blocks. The grounds are accessed from the southern entrance via a network of lanes. All buildings are linked to an underground car park, freeing the site from vehicles above ground. A clubhouse with a pool is located at the northern tip of the site. It follows the irregular shape of the steep hill, forming a retaining wall that defines the border of the property.

RELAXATION

NINETREE VILLAGE'S ORGANIC, FLOWING LAYOUT ENCOURAGES RESIDENTS TO TAKE LONG WALKS THROUGH INVIGORATING GREENERY, WHILE OFFERING PANORAMIC VIEWS FROM ITS LOW-RISE BUILDINGS. ITS INTERIORS PROMOTE PEACE OF MIND AND RELAXATION, CHAMPIONING OPEN SPACES AND ELEGANT SIMPLICITY WITH LUXURIOUS MATERIALS.

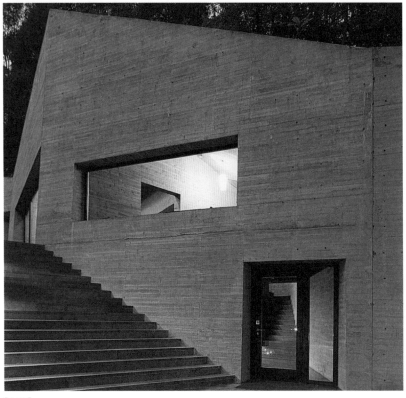

PRENZLAUER GÄRTEN AND PARKPALAIS
STEPHAN HÖHNE GESELLSCHAFT VON ARCHITEKTEN

LOCATION: AM FRIEDRICHSHAIN 26-27 AND 28-32, BERLIN, GERMANY | **COMPLETION:** 2008 AND 2010 | **CLIENT:** PRENZLAUER GÄRTEN GRUNDBESITZ GMBH | **OPEN SPACE PLANNING:** WES & PARTNER LANDSCHAFTSARCHITEKTEN, OFFICE REGINA POLY LANDSCHAFTSARCHITEKTEN | **PHOTOGRAPHER:** STEFAN MÜLLER

Two prestigious gate buildings with a classical residential construction style constitute the entrance to a private road. They are designed as apartments that share a common entrance in groups of two and three. The living areas and loggias on the southern side of the apartments, duplexes and penthouses face Volkspark Friedrichshain, while the bedrooms face away from the street. Behind these gate buildings, 3- and 4-floor townhouses in the English style shaped by John Nash in the 19th century are separately accessible on the mezzanine level by a front yard staircase and create a residential gallery. Each townhouse is equipped with a private garage located in the basement that is accessed via a ramp. The living rooms face the private gardens, while the bedrooms on the upper floors face the gardens and the residential galleries. Behind the new buildings, private patio gardens are bordered by white garden walls. The parkway-style passage with small crowned pear trees bulges out at the center into a generously proportioned park, the "Schweizer Garten". The gallery culminates in two four-story townhouses and the listed Schneider brewery.

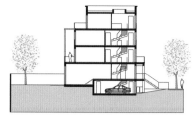

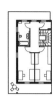

FACTS
SITE SIZE: 15,482 + 1,350 SQM
GFA TOTAL: 15,500 + 3,002 SQM
NO. BUILDINGS: 65 + 1 (PARKPALAIS)
NO. UNITS: 110 + 14
ROAD LENGTH: 271 M
INHABITANTS: 350 + 45
KIND OF UNITS: 1-4 BEDROOMS (GATEHOUSES AND TOWNHOUSES,
PRENZLAUER GÄRTEN) + 1-6 BEDROOMS (PARKPALAIS)
2-STORY UNDERGROUND PARKING FOR 110 CARS AND 10 MOTORBIKES
COMMERCIAL USE (ENTRANCE LEVEL OF PARKPALAIS)

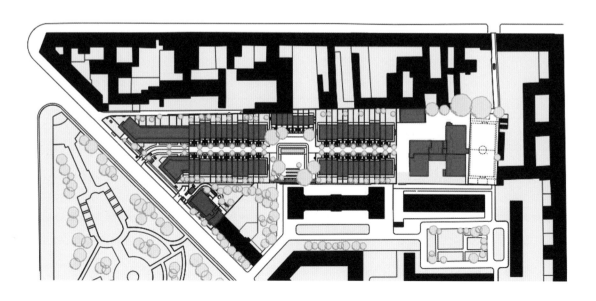

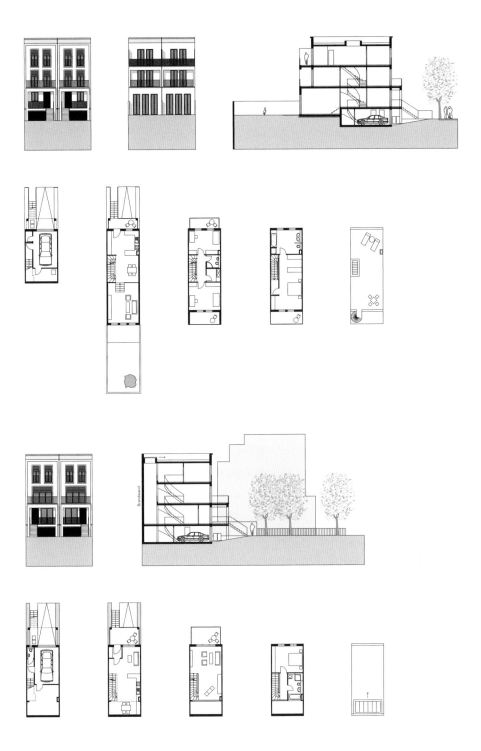

The two sister projects are located at the south-eastern edge of the former Berlin district of Prenzlauer Berg, directly across Volkspark Friedrichshain. Prenzlauer Berg is dominated by urban development structures that were created at the turn of the 20th century. The two projects are harmoniously incorporated into the existing urban structure as a new independent ensemble. They constitute a separate city within the city in the style of urban block galleries such as Riehmers Hofgarten and the Goethepassage in Berlin. Two high head buildings with single-story flats create an entrance gate to a residential street extending deep into the plot with two- to three-story townhouses on both sides. The historic Schneider brewery and the Märchenbrunnen of the Volkspark Friedrichshain are staged as the beginning and end points of the vertically planned urban space.

A SAFE HAVEN IN THE CITY
A PRIVATE STREET, PROTECTED
ACCESS TO THE PREMISES VIA STAIRS
IN THE FRONT YARDS, ACCESS VIA
THE FIRST FLOOR AS WELL AS PRI-
VATE GREEN AREAS AND LEISURE
FACILITIES GUARANTEE THE PRIVACY
OF THE RESIDENTS.

RESIDENTIAL CONVERSION OF THE DENSA PREMISES BASEL
LUCA SELVA ARCHITEKTEN

LOCATION: NEUHAUSSTRASSE 28-36, SALMENWEG 12-16, 4057 BASEL, SWITZERLAND | **COMPLETION:** 2012 | **CLIENT:** DENSA IMMOBILIEN AG | **LANDSCAPE ARCHITECTS:** AUGUST AND MARGRITH KÜNZEL LANDSCHAFTSARCHITEKTEN AG | **PHOTOGRAPHER:** RUEDI WALTI

The two six-floor residential complexes include 99 apartments of various types and characters that each benefit from the open construction character in their own way. Despite the high density, the angular offset buildings offer deliberately created views and diagonal interactive views within the extension. In addition, the geometry and positioning of the building accommodates flexible outdoor spaces that are confined yet flowing open. The peace and quiet that is emanated from the location is supported by the selected materials of self-supportive brickwork, whose varied sur-

faces and deep reveals give the building a strong three-dimensional quality. The windows are located on the level of the inner façade, designed as a white flat casing that is detached from the external walls at the loggias. While the northern building is structured orthogonally on the inside, the southern building is more generously proportioned. As in other projects by the architects, many of the apartments of the Densa complex contain moments of surprise, be it an unexpected view or an interesting path.

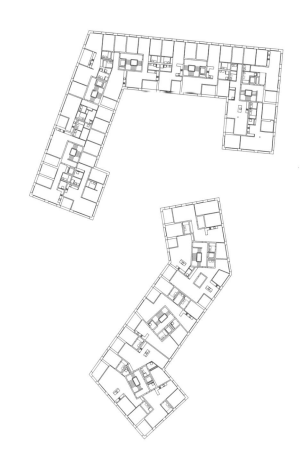

FACTS
SITE SIZE: 8,044 SQM
GFA TOTAL: 13,850 SQM
NO. BUILDINGS: 2
NO. UNITS: 99
ROAD LENGTH: 80 M
INHABITANTS: 220
KIND OF UNITS: 35 DIFFERENT TYPES,
1-4 BEDROOMS
178 UNDERGROUND PARKING LOTS
DAYCARE CENTER, OFFICES, CAR
SHARING

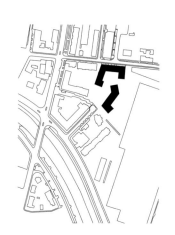

The existing urban development situation is characterized by great fragmentation and heterogeneous structures. The new development cleverly negotiates among the existing perimeter block fragments, individual buildings, and the neighboring large-scale shopping center on the premises of the former dye works. Similar to this plot, the Densa premises were also previously used industrially. The location consists of rows of houses and perimeter block fragments. The theme of the project derives the shape of its two buildings from the analysis of the existing structures. They have different natures, one creating a street space and the other developing freely in the garden space. This creates interesting and varied outdoor spaces that significantly contribute to the development of the specific quality of the location. The typology of the apartments and the materials of the buildings were also related to and dependent on the location. The result is two building structures that differ yet complement each other.

SMOOTH FAÇADES
THE FAÇADES THAT ARE INTER-
CEPTED BY LARGE RECTANGULAR
OPENINGS CONSIST OF SELF-
SUPPORTIVE EXPOSED CLINKER
BRICKWORK. AS THESE ONLY
VARY IN THEIR WIDTH BUT NOT
THEIR HEIGHT, THE FAÇADE AP-
PEARS VERY SMOOTH AND EVEN.

WOHNPARK HORASBRÜCKE
STURM UND WARTZECK

LOCATION: HORASBRÜCKE 2-7, 36039 FULDA, GERMANY | **COMPLETION:** 2014 | **CLIENT:** SIEDLUNGSWERK FULDA EG | **OPEN SPACE DESIGN:** PLANUNGSBÜRO HERGET **PHOTOGRAPHER:** FOTODESIGN WOLFGANG FALLIER

The shown layout variations are all based on apartment widths of 5.3 and 6.7 meters. The access core with elevators and stairs is always situated at the center. The ground floor apartments that are located on the outside each have a separate side entrance. Similar to a modular system, different residence sizes and layouts could be selected and combined in the planning phase (apartments, duplexes, townhouses, penthouses). The layouts could thus be adjusted to the demand of the three construction phases. A 6.7-meter-wide unit on the ground floor offers storage space for the community of residents, for instance for basement substitution and bicycle parking. The three-story buildings are built as a massive construction with walls made of highly insulated honeycomb bricks. The monolithic construction style with white plastered façades was implemented without a thermal insulation compound system while the areas with more mechanical wear such as the entrances and the garbage containers were implemented with a clinker facing to ensure the long service life and economical maintenance of the façades. The windows consist of timber-aluminum elements and the large-scale glazing of the penthouses feature a mullion and transom design.

FACTS

SITE SIZE: 8,180 SQM
GFA TOTAL: 5,940 SQM
NO. BUILDINGS: 6
NO. UNITS: 44
ROAD LENGTH: 200 M
INHABITANTS: 90
KIND OF UNITS: APARTMENTS 55–130
SQM, MAISONETTES, PENTHOUSES,
TERRACED HOUSES
48 PARKING LOTS

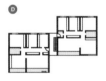   

   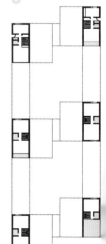

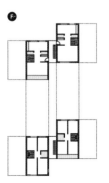 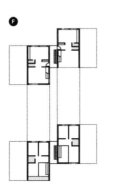  

The residential complex with 44 rental apartments is located on the edge of the core city of Fulda, underneath the Frauenberg. It is framed to the north-west by a high railway embankment and to the north-east and south-east by existing buildings. To the south-east it borders the open areas of the Fulda wetlands. To ensure responsible handling of the silhouette of the Frauenberg and its Wilhelminian era villas, the height of the flat roofs of the buildings is adjusted

accordingly while their colors are matched to the white villa architecture. The urban development composition of the buildings pays tribute to the local volumes through projections and recesses. The prominent incisions of the outdoor seating provides a rhythm to the entire ensemble, giving it a unique character.

MODULAR COMBINATION
SIMILAR TO A MODULAR SYSTEM, DIFFERENT RESIDENCE SIZES AND LAYOUTS COULD BE SELECTED AND COMBINED IN THE PLANNING PHASE: APARTMENTS, DUPLEXES, TOWN-HOUSES AND PENTHOUSES UNITE IN ONE RESIDENTIAL ESTATE.

ELY COURT
ALISON BROOKS ARCHITECTS

LOCATION: CHICHESTER ROAD, KILBURN, LONDON NW6, ENGLAND | **COMPLETION:** 2015 | **CLIENT:** LONDON BOROUGH OF BRENT & CATALYST HOUSING | **LANDSCAPE ARCHITECTS:** CHURCHMAN LANDSCAPE ARCHITECTS, ADAMS HAEBERMEHL | **PHOTOGRAPHER:** PAUL RIDDLE

This 43-dwelling residential development is intended as a catalyst for social and urban transformation, a modern interpretation of 19th century housing typologies and street patterns. Ely Court consists of four building types, each with a different scale and organization, responding to its specific locale. The Terrace is an interpretation of neighboring Maida Vale's 19th century mansion blocks – with two-floor duplexes on the ground floor and apartments above, it features front porticos, upper porticos and recessed balconies, resulting in highly articulated, rhythmic façades.

The Mews consists of eight houses that introduce a finer grain of development to the scheme, with a serrated roofscape that allows sunlight into the street. The Flatiron and Link Block frame the new garden square in front of the 1960s Alpha House, acting as sentinels overlooking the park.

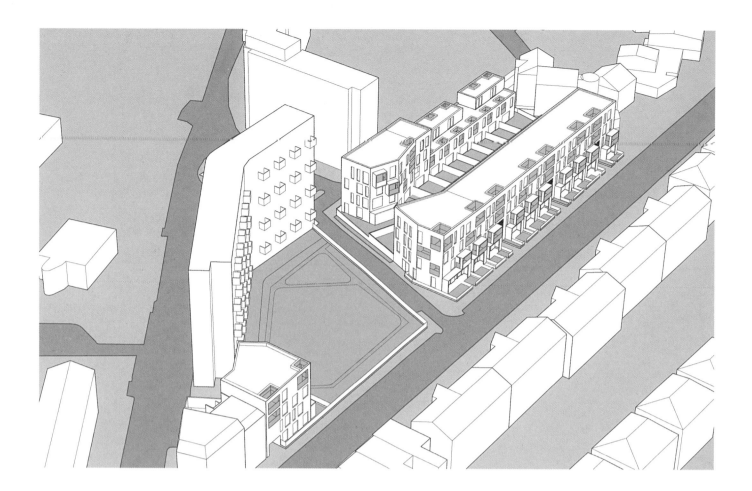

FACTS
SITE SIZE: 6,380 SQM
GFA TOTAL: 6,509 SQM
NO. BUILDINGS: 4
NO. UNITS: 43
ROAD LENGTH: 260 M
INHABITANTS: 163
KIND OF UNITS: APARTMENTS, MAISONETTES, MEWS HOUSES
46 PARKING LOTS

The project is part of the South Kilburn Estate regeneration master plan for the London borough of Brent. Ely Court represents 150 years of London's urban evolution. The site is part of the South Kilburn Estate, one of London's largest post-war renewal programs. Tower blocks and car parks are surrounded by open green space. Mid-19th century semi-detached villas, 1960s flat blocks, a Salvation Army Center, and a former pub border the site. Alison Brooks Architects' site master plan reinstates the block and street pattern that characterized this 19th-century London "suburb" before its post-war redevelopment. A new mews draws pedestrians and vehicles into what was previously an isolated and under-used "green space" between slab blocks and acts as a spine between two new developments.

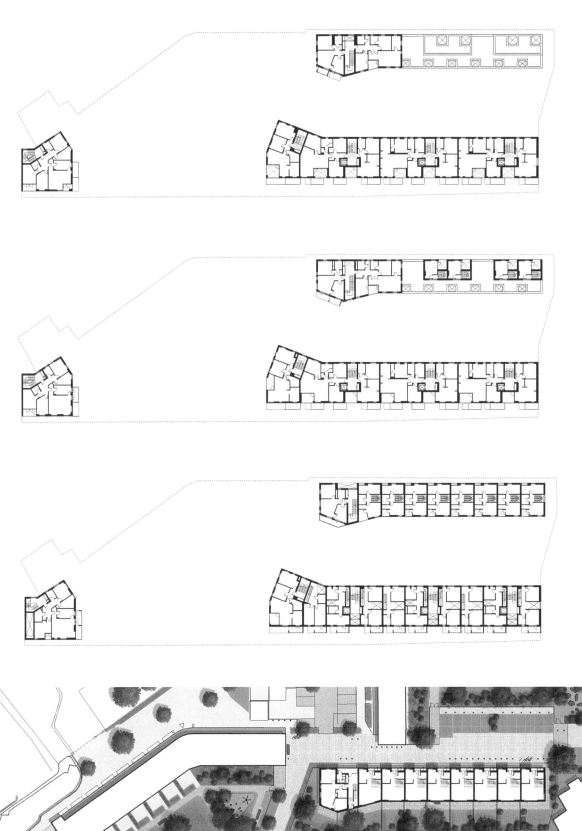

REINSTATING STREET LIFE

STREET LIFE IS RE-ANIMATING AND INTEGRATING A DENSER FORMAT OF SOCIAL HOUSING INTO THE FABRIC OF A NORTH LONDON NEIGHBORHOOD BY REINSTATING THE HISTORIC BLOCK PATTERN AND BY INTRODUCING PORTICOS, BALCONIES, AND PORCHES THAT EMBRACE THE PUBLIC SPACE OF THE STREET.

WOHNSIEDLUNG WERDWIES
ADRIAN STREICH ARCHITEKTEN

LOCATION: GRÜNAURING 25-37, BÄNDLISTRASSE 22-34, 8064 ZURICH, SWITZERLAND | **COMPLETION:** 2007 | **CLIENT:** CITY OF ZURICH | **LANDSCAPE DESIGN:** SCHMID LANDSCHAFTSARCHITEKTEN | **PHOTOGRAPHER:** ROGER FREI (256-257), ROLAND BERNATH (252-253)

In line with the public character of the outdoor spaces of the residential complex Werdwies, the ground floor contains a wholesale food retailer, a bistro, smaller commercial spaces, two kindergartens, and a day nursery. These public services contribute significantly to the infrastructure of the quarter on the edge of the city. All 152 apartments with 2-6 rooms are located on the upper floors. Each apartment consists of a variably illuminated sequence of living, dining, and bedrooms. Simple layouts with long rooms, wall-filling fitted closets and generous loggias give the apartments a robust charm that appeals to a wide audience. With their seemingly simple architectural language, the apartments provide a quiet backdrop for the lively public squares. When looked at in detail, it appears that the design is very sophisticated while the windows are arranged in such a way as to constitute a varied pattern of perforation with various perspective insights.

FACTS
SITE SIZE: 15,353 SQM
GFA TOTAL: 32,313 SQM
NO. BUILDINGS: 7
NO. UNITS: 152
ROAD LENGTH: 268 M
INHABITANTS: 500
KIND OF UNITS: 1–5 BEDROOMS
136 PARKING LOTS IN MULTI-STORY
CAR PARK
28 MUSIC ROOMS, FOOD SHOP, BISTRO,
SEVERAL SMALLER COMMERCIAL
PREMISES, NURSERY, KINDERGARTEN

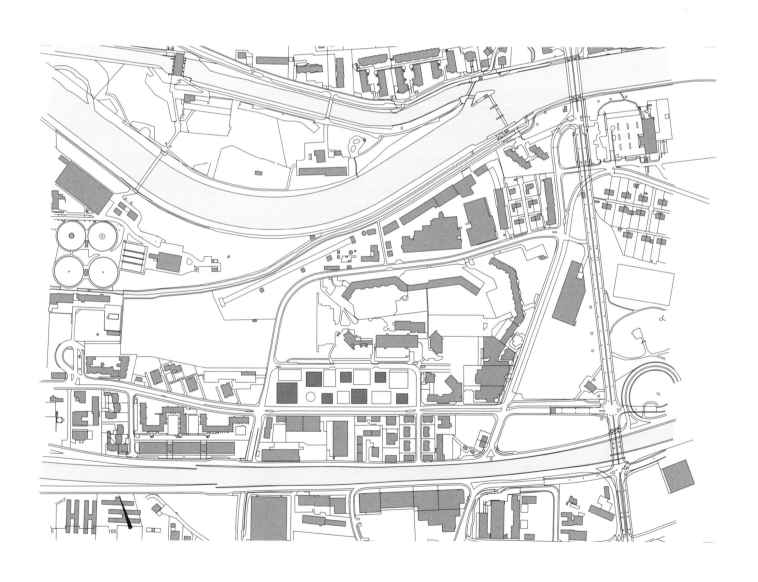

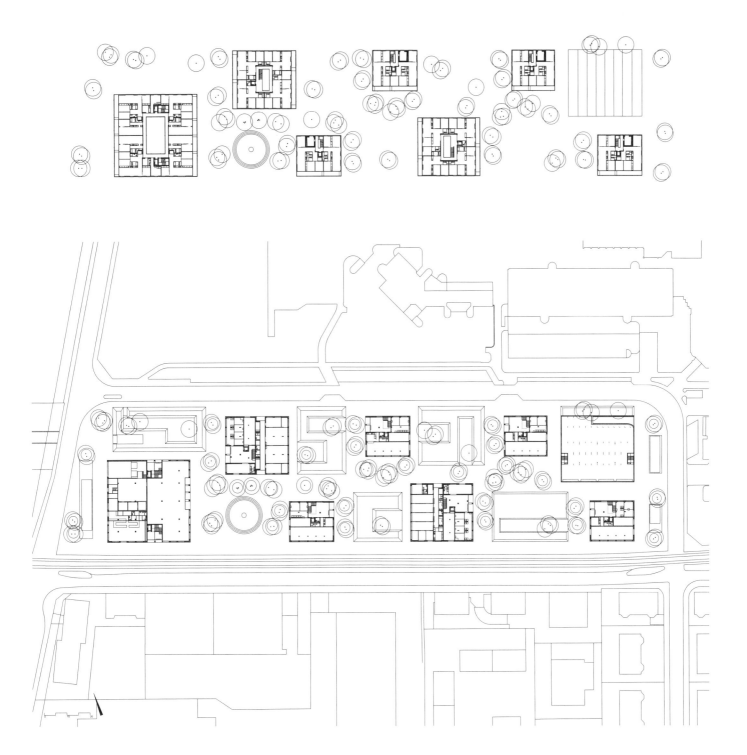

On the western edge of Zurich, the quiet course of the river Limmat and the noisy highway are juxtaposed like antipodes, surrounding the island-like macrocosm of the Grünau quarter. Wohnsiedlung Werdwies provides the quarter with an open center coupled with high spatial density. Seven rectangular apartment blocks are arranged along Grünauring and Bändlistrasse, creating an alternating rhythm of filled and empty spaces. Among the houses emerge smaller and larger squares that open up towards the quarter. This open structure interweaves with the extensive green areas to the north and the parceled quarter structure to the south. This gives the Grünau quarter a comprehensive spatial connection.

SPACE AND DENSITY
THE RESIDENTIAL SETTLEMENT PROVIDES THE QUARTER WITH AN OPEN CENTER COUPLED WITH HIGH SPATIAL DENSITY. SEVEN RECTANGULAR APARTMENT BLOCKS ARE ARRANGED ALONG GRÜNAURING AND BÄNDLI-STRASSE, CREATING AN ALTER-NATING RHYTHM OF FILLED AND EMPTY SPACES.

LB CAMDEN AGAR GROVE ESTATE
HAWKINS\BROWN | MAE ARCHITECTS | GRANT ASSOCIATES

LOCATION: AGAR GROVE, LONDON NW1 0RE, ENGLAND | **COMPLETION:** ONGOING |
CLIENT: LONDON BOROUGH OF CAMDEN | **VISUALIZATION:** FORBES MASSIE,
HAWKINS\BROWN (260, 261)

The main move of the Agar Grove redevelopment is "growing the grove" – to re-link an isolated modernist housing estate with its Victorian context. The first step will be replacing the existing pattern of dead end routes and poor connectivity with a coherent network of streets and squares; stitching the scheme back into the local urban fabric. New streets will provide pedestrian, cycle and vehicle access to the estate.

Agar Grove will become a safe family neighborhood surrounded by streets with continuous well-defined blocks and active fronts. The second step, refurbishing Lulworth Tower, shall improve its sustainability and identity. Throughout, well built homes of high quality and with very good standards of environmental performance will be constructed. At the heart of the scheme will be a new garden square. The range of building scales provides a variety of spaces around the central tower. The landscape design strengthens the character of each space, as well as providing year-round color, scent and delight. It supports a comprehensive sustainable urban drainage system (SUDs), while on the roof garden a mosaic of habitat types promotes biodiversity, using various species to support Camden targets. The scheme is based on a mix of building types, including terrace, villa, mansion, and tower, to create diversity in type, scale and appearance.

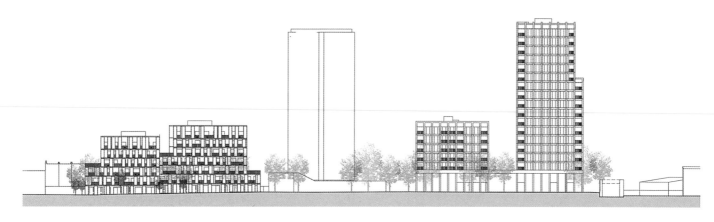

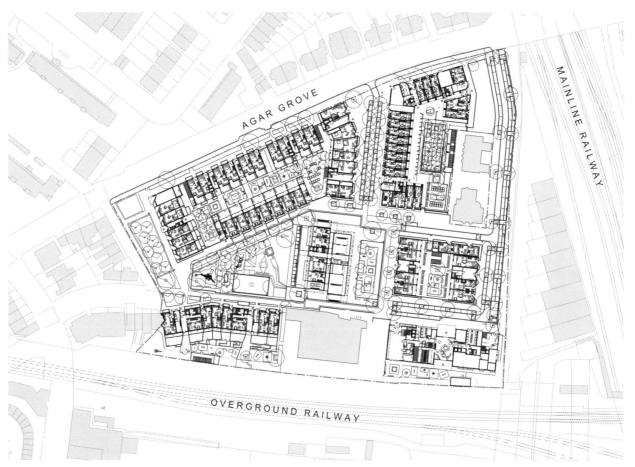

FACTS
SITE SIZE: 27,500 SQM
GFA TOTAL: 55,000 SQM
NO. BUILDINGS: 10
NO. UNITS: 493
ROAD LENGTH: 385 M
INHABITANTS: 1,664
KIND OF UNITS: 1-4-BEDROOM APARTMENTS, MAISONETTES
CHILDREN'S CENTER

Hawkins\Brown with Mae Architects and Grant Associates designed the UK's largest passive house scheme for the local housing authority, London Borough of Camden, in the north of Inner London. The original Agar Grove Estate was constructed in 1966 on a site adjacent to two railway lines in the modernist style as a social housing project. It comprised 249 homes arranged in a series of low-rise blocks clustered around an eighteen-story tower (Lulworth Tower) served by its own shop and café. The buildings were in poor condition and the public space was dilapidated and under-used. The residents' brief was to demolish 110 homes, retain 140 homes, and provide 360 new homes. This redevelopment project will be completely self-funding with market sale revenue funding the affordable housing.

IDENTITY BY LANDMARKS
A CONSCIOUS AND CONSIDERED DECISION WAS MADE TO RETAIN LULWORTH TOWER AT THE CENTER OF THE SCHEME, TO STRIP IT BACK TO ITS STRUCTURAL FRAME AND EXTEND IT UPWARDS BY TWO FLOORS, ADDING GLAZED BALCONIES, A FEATURE THAT IT HAD LACKED PREVIOUSLY. THIS PRESERVED THE SITE'S LANDMARK AND ENSURED THE TOWER'S COMMERCIAL VIABILITY.

SHANGHAI WORLD EXPO VILLAGE
HPP INTERNATIONAL

LOCATION: SHIBOCUN ROAD, PUDONG, SHANGHAI, CHINA | **COMPLETION:** 2010 | **CLIENT:** SHANGHAI WORLD EXPO LAND HOLDING CO., LTD. | **PHOTOGRAPHER:** JOCHEN HELLE

The multi-faceted pattern of use of the Expo Village in Shanghai includes a hotel and residential buildings along with retail, cultural and leisure facilities. The modular concept accommodates residential units ranging from 30 to 250 square meters. For climate control reasons, the individual buildings are aligned from north to south. Combined with the offset linear placement of the buildings, this orientation also offers optimized views of the river and the city. Following the Expo, during which the complex served as accommodations for staff and visitors, the quarter has become a new and dynamic city quarter that is harmoniously integrated into Shanghai's city structure. Based on a flexibly designed construction grid and easily al-

terable patterns of use, the subsequent reuse of the buildings was planned from the outset. The design of the Expo Village was based on the construction structures and shapes of large European cities. As the surrounding areas of Shanghai are heterogeneous and dominated by solitary buildings, the main focus was on the grown structures and stone façades of European quarters. The pre-constructed perforated stone façades of the Expo Village convey stability and peace inside the mostly glazed Shanghai cityscape, while ensuring sustainable energy. Due to the massive construction style, cooling and air conditioning could be reduced to a minimum, thus the Expo Village can be seen as a model for adequately handling resources.

FACTS

SITE SIZE: 440,000 SQM
GFA TOTAL: 700,000 SQM
NO. BUILDINGS: 24
ROAD LENGTH: 1.82 KM
KIND OF UNITS: APARTMENTS AND
PENTHOUSES (PARTLY SERVICED),
MULTI-FAMILY RESIDENCES, SCAL-
ABLE 30-350 SQM
1,854 UNDERGROUND PARKING LOTS
286 PARKING LOTS ABOVE GROUND
900-ROOM LUXURY HOTEL, BUDGET
HOTEL, OFFICES, LOGISTICS, RETAIL
AND ENTERTAINMENT FACILITIES,
RESTORED FACTORY

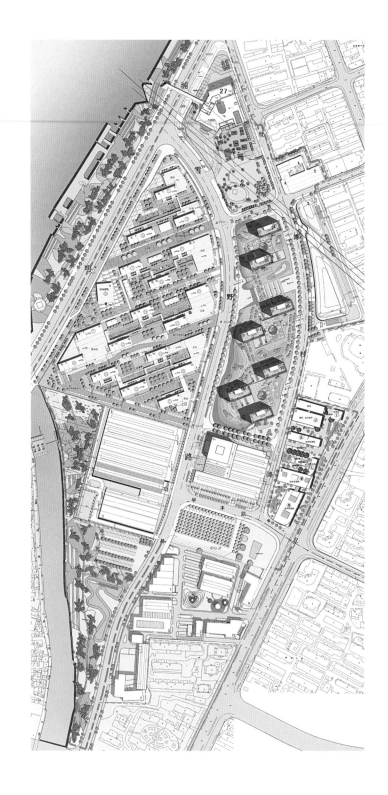

The Expo Village was created on the occasion of the Expo Shanghai in 2010 on a 44-hectare planning area in the north-east of the Pudong district. The new quarter on the banks of the Huang Pu river is an outstanding example for the sustainable conversion of existing inner city commercial wastelands into urban city districts with high living quality.

The official theme of the expo "Better City, Better Life", was also the guiding principle for the architectural considerations. Sustainable planning commences in high-density urban situations with the balanced allocation of empty and constructed areas. In addition to a gross floor space of 700,000 square meters, the Expo Village also contains approximately 16 hectares of park areas that are connected to the surrounding landscape, the bank of the Huang Pu, the urban surrounding, and the planned construction structure.

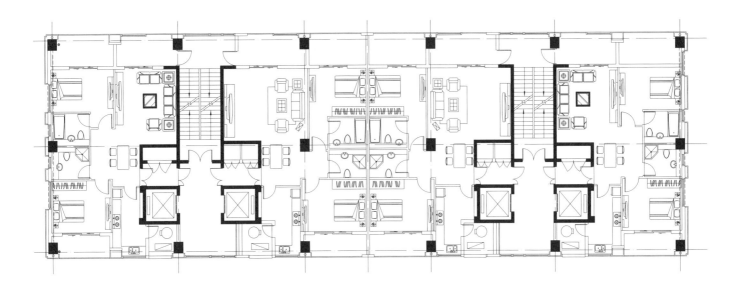

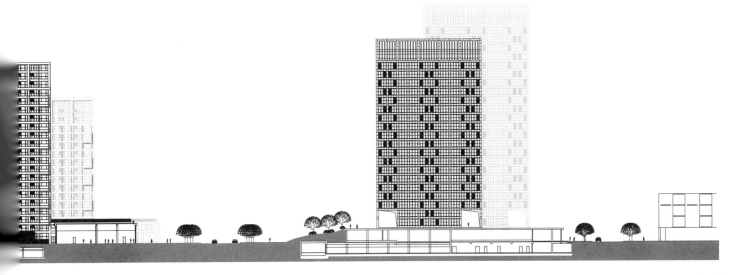

FOLLOW-UP AND NEW USES
A FLEXIBLE CONSTRUCTION GRID COUPLED WITH MODULAR PLANNING ALLOWED THE PROBLEM-FREE REUSE OF THE EXPO VILLAGE AS A HOTEL, BUSINESS, CULTURE, LEISURE AND RESIDENTIAL QUARTER.

INDEX